Stadium Stories:
Michigan State Spartans

Stadium Stories™ Series

Stadium Stories:
Michigan State Spartans

Joe Rexrode

INSIDERS' GUIDE®

GUILFORD, CONNECTICUT
AN IMPRINT OF THE GLOBE PEQUOT PRESS

INSIDERS' GUIDE®

Copyright © 2006 by Morris Book Publishing, LLC

Insiders' Guide is a registered trademark of Morris Book Publishing, LLC.
Stadium Stories is a trademark of Morris Book Publishing, LLC.

Text design: Casey Shain

All photos courtesy of MSU Sports Information, unless otherwise noted.

Cover photos: *front cover:* Drew Stanton; *back cover:* top, Duffy Daugherty and MSU's 1966 All-Americans; bottom, Marc Renaud against Michigan.

Library of Congress Cataloging-in-Publication Data

Rexrode, Joe.
    Stadium stories : Michigan State Spartans / Joe Rexrode. — 1st ed.
    p. cm. — (Stadium stories series)
    ISBN-13: 978-0-7627-4027-7
    ISBN-10: 0-7627-4027-2
    1. Michigan State University—Football—History. 2. Michigan State Spartans (Football team)—History. I. Title. II. Series.
GV958.M5R49 2006
796.332'630977427—dc22   2006041815

Manufactured in the United States of America
First Edition/First Printing

For Katie, who offered encouragement, patience, and hard editing at all the right times.

Contents

Acknowledgments

A number of people helped me put this book together, none more important than Paulette Martis in Michigan State's Sports Information Department. For your extended assistance, Paulette, I will forever be grateful.

Several others aided along the way, including *Lansing State Journal* executive editor Mickey Hirten, sports editor Brent Neal, and librarians Diana Buchanan and Pam Gawronski; MSU associate athletic director John Lewandowski; Tim Staudt; Tony Conley; Mike Rosenberg; and Jemele Hill. I would also like to acknowledge the late Fred Stabley's book *The Spartans* for providing inspiration.

Finally, a hearty thanks to the dozens of members of the MSU football family who took the time to speak with me.

All Aggies

Bonfires roared and revelers danced. At least one building burned to the ground that Saturday night in East Lansing, Michigan. A celebration unlike anything the area had witnessed stretched 4 miles west to the state capitol building in Lansing.

It was October 18, 1913. For the first time in eight tries, Michigan Agricultural College had achieved a football victory over the University of Michigan. A lopsided relationship had become a rivalry, and the state's tiny "cow college," as it was popularly known in those days, had earned itself some respect.

Coach John Macklin's upstart Aggies had used power and innovation to topple Fielding Yost's mighty Wolverines 12–7 in Ann Arbor. It was a stunner the *Detroit Times* called "among the biggest upsets in college football history," and with good reason. In the series's previous seven contests, MAC had been outscored 280–13, including a 55–7 humiliation in 1912.

A crowd of 8,509, wearing suits, hats, and dresses and paying a buck apiece, took in the action on a crisp, sunny day at Michigan's Ferry Field. About a thousand of those had boarded trains that morning in East Lansing due for Ann Arbor to root on their Aggies.

What they saw was a brutally violent game, one that had been built up with pregame trash talk in the newspapers; secretive, heavily guarded night practices for Macklin's squad; and a massive student rally that galvanized MAC like nothing before.

They also witnessed a dominant performance from first-year MAC tackle Gideon Smith, one of the first African Americans to play college football. And they saw the Aggies hurt the Wolverines repeatedly with the forward pass, an element of the game that most still considered a novelty. (It was two weeks later, on November 1, that Notre Dame used it—with Gus Dorais throwing to Knute Rockne—to upset Army in an oft-romanticized exhibition that made the pass fashionable.)

When it was over, the Michigan faithful could only sit and watch as MAC's fans rushed the field and lifted the players onto their shoulders for a thirty-minute parade of sorts, then spilled into Ann Arbor for more. The Aggies did not yet have a fight song, so MAC's ROTC cadet band marched through the streets playing Michigan's famed anthem, "The Victors."

Evolution of a Name

Forty-one years after Michigan Agricultural College was established as the nation's first federal land-grant institution, football made its competitive debut on campus. The MAC Aggies opened play September 26, 1896, with a rousing 10–0 triumph—over Lansing High School.

In those early years, newspaper accounts often referred to the Aggies as the "Fighting Farmers," although that was never an official title. In 1925 MAC, having expanded tremendously from its all-agriculture beginnings, became Michigan State College. The college then sponsored a contest to find a nickname to replace "Aggies."

When the school chose "Michigan Staters" as the winner, longtime *Lansing State Journal* sports editor George S. Alderton was neither impressed nor particularly excited about the prospect of writing about the Michigan State Michigan Staters. So Alderton combed through some of the losing entries and ran across "Spartans."

Alderton began using "Spartans" in baseball stories in April 1926, and by the 1926 football season, everyone was using it. "It began appearing in other newspapers," he explained later. "And when the student publication used it, that clinched it."

MSC changed its name to Michigan State University in 1955—completing a one-hundred-year journey from MAC Aggies to MSU Spartans.

It had never sounded so good to Macklin's team of twelve, the eight hundred accompanying students, and two hundred other rooters, many of them MAC faculty members. They all boarded trains early that evening, due back in East Lansing at 11:00 that night. When they arrived, the party was well under way. Anyone who thinks this country wasn't yet sports-crazed in the early twentieth century hasn't peered at the events surrounding this game.

In 1913 Americans were introduced to the income tax and their twenty-eighth president, Woodrow Wilson. Henry Ford had just developed the first moving assembly line, and the Athletics (Philadelphia, not Oakland) beat the Giants (New York, not San Francisco) in the World Series. A great war, later to be dubbed World War I, was brewing. It would be set into full motion on June 28, 1914, when Serbian assassin Gavrilo Princip gunned down Austrian Archduke Franz Ferdinand in Sarajevo.

Back in East Lansing, nine months before Princip's fateful shots, MAC's football team was preparing for its eighteenth season with high anticipation. College football's burgeoning popularity was mirrored at MAC, where Macklin had gone 12–2 in his first two seasons.

MAC's football program, started in 1896, got serious when Chester Brewer arrived to coach in 1903. Brewer, a four-sport star at Wisconsin, was hired to replace George Denman a year after Yost's Wolverines humiliated MAC 119–0. He quickly legitimized the MAC program. Brewer's greatest successes were a 0–0 tie with Michigan in 1908 and a 17–0 upset of Notre Dame, which featured freshmen Dorais and Rockne, in 1910.

When Brewer left to coach Missouri after the 1910 campaign, MAC president Jonathan L. Snyder hired John Macklin,

John Macklin was a giant man (6'7", 275 pounds) who turned MAC into a big-time program in his five seasons as head coach.

a massive man who had starred on the gridiron at Ivy League power Penn. His size (6'7", 275 pounds by one account) enhanced an intimidating presence during demanding practices. Macklin was said to be a masterful motivator and tireless tinkerer, and he brought with him an increased emphasis on the pass, which had been legalized in 1906.

Macklin got immediate results, the most significant of which was a 35–20 win at Ohio State to close the 1912 season. It was MAC's first win over a team from the Big Ten (which would not welcome Michigan State into its ranks until 1948) and an indication that the Aggies were playing at a new level.

MAC welcomed back a host of talented returnees for the 1913 season, including quarterback George Gauthier, end Blake Miller, fullback George "Carp" Julian, and left tackle Chester Gifford, the team's captain. Newcomers Hugh Blacklock, a halfback, and Gideon Smith, a forceful right tackle, made the difference for what would become MAC's first perfect season.

Smith, of Norfolk County, Virginia, was a transfer student from Ferris State who had tried out for the MAC team in 1912. Macklin had misgivings at first, but Smith showed enough in a tryout to stay on as a practice player. He officially became part of the team in 1913—making him the third recorded African American to play college football. He would later be the first black man to graduate from MAC and one of the first to play pro football.

On road trips, Smith couldn't eat or stay with the rest of the team, so Macklin would give him a few bucks, and Smith would reappear in time for pregame warm-ups. During games Smith withstood racially charged verbal abuse from across the line that, Miller said years later, "couldn't be printed."

Pigskin Pioneer

Jackie Robinson became the first black major league baseball player in 1947. That same year, Gideon Smith returned to Michigan State to earn a graduate degree—thirty-four years after he had become the school's first black athlete.

Smith was a dominant, 6'2", 180-pound tackle for three seasons (1913–15) at what was then called Michigan Agricultural College, and his teams went 17–3, including 2–1 against Michigan. The citizens of Lansing gave him a gold watch after his senior season in appreciation of the way he handled racism-fueled adversity on and off the field.

Smith served in World War I and then went on to be one of the first African Americans to play pro football, teaming up for two seasons with the Canton Bulldogs and Jim Thorpe. After one game Thorpe told Smith: "I wish you were in there all the time. They don't pay quite so much attention to me when you're in the game."

"I guess that was the nicest compliment I ever had, coming from an athlete like Jim Thorpe," Smith told the *Lansing State Journal* in 1947.

The Virginia native became head football coach at Hampton Institute in 1921, a position he held for thirty-four years. Smith died in 1968 at age seventy-nine. He is a charter member of the National Football Foundation Hall of Fame.

Gideon Smith starred in MAC's first two wins over Michigan.

But Smith hung in and steadily became a force, especially as a run-stuffing defender. Tackles and guards were still allowed to carry the ball, and on offense Macklin occasionally got Smith the ball on "tackle around" plays to utilize his speed and power.

That oddity aside, the game was rapidly evolving to resemble its modern form. The thirty-five-minute halves of the early twentieth century were now fifteen-minute quarters. A first down required 10 yards, up from 5. In 1912 a host of changes were made to the game: The field was shortened from 110 to 100 yards; a fourth down was added; touchdowns increased in value from 5 points to 6; and kickoffs were moved back from midfield to the kicking team's 40 (although teams still *received* the ball after scoring, sort of like a make-it-take-it basketball game).

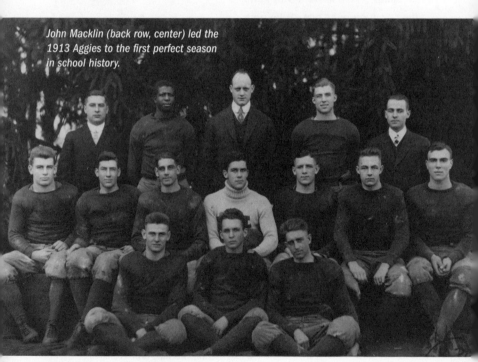

John Macklin (back row, center) led the 1913 Aggies to the first perfect season in school history.

The Aggies opened 1913 by whipping a pair of in-state schools. Olivet fell 26–0 in the opener, followed by Alma, 57–0, the next week. Next up was Michigan and a week of anticipation that would rival anything seen on today's campuses.

Yost had arrived at Michigan in 1901 and immediately turned the Wolverines into one of the nation's premier programs. He became a bona fide villain around the Lansing area when, in 1902, his second U-M team rolled up a 119–0 margin on the Aggies.

Six years later, MAC earned a cherished tie against Yost, and two years after that, in 1910, the Aggies fell 6–3 in a loss they blamed on several questionable calls by the officials. MAC was starting to catch up, and the bitterness that continues to mark the series was beginning to surface.

The 1913 hype began well before game week. In a *Lansing State Journal* story on Wednesday, October 8—three days before the Wolverines took on Mount Union and the Aggies played Alma—former Michigan player George "Bottles" Thomson proclaimed that the Wolverines would stomp the Aggies by 35 points.

Two days later, former MAC player Elmer "Chill" Gorenflo responded. Gorenflo, then a part-time assistant for the Aggies, had scouted Michigan's season-opening win against Case. "MAC has just as good or a better team than they have and should come out at the top of the heap," he told the *State Journal*. "So far as I have been able to dope it out, all Michigan has this year is a name. I wonder if Bottles Thomson has any money to back that 35–0 prediction of his."

After the Alma victory, MAC began its preparations for

Michigan in earnest. "Secret Practice for Aggies this Week Ordered," proclaimed a *State Journal* headline on October 14.

Macklin cut off the usual public access to practice, fearing U-M spies. He was so concerned, he had armed ROTC members stand watch. Even the familiar faces of fellow students and young fans from the area had to stay away. "The east side of the Cedar River was the nearest the worshippers of the Aggies approached their idols," wrote the *State Journal*'s Don O. Champney.

That week's practices extended well into the evening, under lights Macklin had installed. He excused his players one by one, waiting until he was fully satisfied with each man's effort. Macklin also made a strategic adjustment, moving star end Blake Miller to left halfback, in hopes of throwing off U-M's defense.

Meanwhile, the MAC campus buzzed with anticipation. A massive pep rally took place the evening of Thursday, October 16. An estimated crowd of 1,500 students showed up, the largest gathering at the school to date—total enrollment that semester was 1,643. In other words, about 91 percent of the student body came to the pep rally. Imagine that kind of attendance today. The event featured several rousing speeches, along with a poem from student Donald Francisco, whose words indicated early hostility over U-M's "cow college" quips:

> *Where did we get our team?*
> *Oh, what a husky eleven,*
> *Who's the teacher of our team?*
> *Macklin, six feet seven,*
> *And don't you start to prattle,*
> *We'll make your bones rattle,*

Lead us, lead us, lead us to the battle,
What is your claim, that we're rubes?
We're thrashing, we're thrashing,
And when we get to crashing,
There'll be some awful smashing,
By heck, won't we celebrate.

Not exactly Walt Whitman, but prophetic. The Aggies were about to earn a celebration with sixty minutes of eye-gouging football.

Kickoff was set for 2:30. The thousand or so MAC fans who spent $2.46 apiece for a round-trip train ticket settled into their seats at Ferry Field. Another thousand stood outside the *State Journal* in downtown Lansing, 60 miles away. The newspaper had promised earlier that week to "megaphone each move of the contesting elevens to the street." The play-by-play account would be telegraphed to the paper from the Ferry Field press box and then relayed to the crowd outside.

MAC won the coin toss and immediately drove deep into Michigan territory, but a fourth-down pass failed and the Wolverines took over. The Aggies' primary weakness was their field goal kicking. Everyone on the team had given it a try, but MAC missed an astounding 75 percent of its extra-point attempts in 1913. So the Aggies typically went for it on fourth down near their opponent's goal line.

Yost, meanwhile, was notorious for punting at the slightest hint of trouble—often on first down if U-M had the ball in its own end of the field. He preferred to play field position and wait for his opponents to make a mistake.

No one was surprised when the Wolverines lined up for a punt on their first play. But U-M faked and gained 5 yards on a run. On the next play, Yost's team was penalized 15 yards for holding, and this time he decided to kick for real, on second-and-20.

The ball was shanked, going out of bounds at U-M's 25. MAC drove again, but Carp Julian, the bruising fullback, came up just shy of a first down on the Michigan 5, and the Wolverines took over there. On first down, George Gauthier, the slippery 5'6" quarterback, returned U-M's punt 3 yards to the Wolverines' 35.

This time the Aggies would make good behind Gauthier's arm. He connected on two straight passes, getting the ball to the U-M 3 yard line. From there, Julian rammed it in for a 6–0 lead.

MAC fullback George "Carp" Julian plunges into the end zone for the first score of the game.

Miller missed the point after, as usual, but it was clear that Yost's defense was having trouble with the pass.

"Today's game is another demonstration of the fact that Yost's men are unable to cope with a team that uses the forward pass for its principle offensive work," wrote the *Detroit Tribune*, in a game story accompanied by a photo of Gauthier setting up to throw, with the heading "Making Michigan Look Foolish." Gauthier ended up connecting on seven of nineteen passes for 100 yards. Those were astounding numbers, considering that the ball in those days was much fatter and more difficult to grip than today's version.

Still, despite Gauthier's success, MAC would not score again on offense. The Wolverines were able to stiffen when they needed a stop, repeatedly turning back the Aggies near the goal line. U-M would also benefit from the loss of one of MAC's top players. Late in the second quarter, Blake Miller ran for 8 yards on a fake punt. He was down when Michigan quarterback Ernest Hughitt raced over—from 20 yards away, by some accounts—and landed on Miller's neck with both knees.

Miller was knocked unconscious and was feared to have a broken neck. He was taken to nearby Homeopathic Hospital, where he woke up three hours later. Luckily for him, the injury turned out to be less serious than originally thought, and he was back with the team the next week.

But on this day, Miller's absence threatened to derail the Aggies just as they were closing in on a landmark win. The sophomore was the team's primary kicker and an elusive runner with the ball. As a senior in 1915, he and fullback Jerry DaPrato would become MAC's first All-Americans.

Up 6–0 at the half, the Aggies were thinking about their lost star. Their lone active reserve, Hewitt Miller—Blake's little brother—would have to come in and try to fill his sibling's shoes. No one would have predicted that he would be one of the game's heroes.

It was quite clear, however, that Gideon Smith would hold that distinction in the case of a MAC victory. He was a terror at tackle, especially on defense, repeatedly disrupting U-M's blocking schemes and stopping Yost's running plays cold. He was the primary reason MAC controlled the line despite giving up an average of 25 pounds per man up front.

"Smith had arms that seemed to be ten feet long, plus the agility of a cat," wrote the *Detroit Times.* "When a play came through the position, he folded up the whole side of the opposing line as if he were playing an accordion."

Yost's offense was bottled up, and things looked especially bleak for his Wolverines early in the third quarter, when U-M fumbled near midfield on a fake punt. Hewitt Miller, fresh into the game at left halfback, scooped up the ball and raced 46 yards for a score, untouched. The Aggies had a commanding 12–0 lead.

But Michigan finally got the break it needed midway through the fourth quarter. Gauthier muffed another of Yost's first down punts, and U-M's Clyde Bastian recovered it and ran 40 yards for a touchdown. The extra point made it 12–7, with plenty of time for the Wolverines to eke out a victory.

The Wolverines received the kickoff and returned the ball to their own 46. Great position for a winning drive—but not good enough for Yost, who promptly punted on first down. Gauthier caught the ball at the 10 and ripped off a 31-yard return, out to the 41.

It appeared Yost's strategy had backfired, but the Wolverines held on for three plays and forced MAC to kick. Dutch Lenardson, punting in place of the injured Blake Miller, put one out of bounds at U-M's 36.

With the clock winding down, Yost pulled a trick out of his bag. End Miller Pontius got the ball on an end around and heaved it downfield. The other end, John Lyons, hauled it in for a 34-yard gain to MAC's 30. The Ann Arbor crowd sensed a stirring comeback.

But the Wolverines were suffering from the game's physical toll. Halfback James Catlett had already been forced from the game with a feared spinal injury (later determined to be a shoulder strain). And now U-M quarterback Ernest Hughitt—"groggy from the hard pounding he had received," said the *Detroit Times*—was forced from the game at the most crucial point. Inexperienced reserve Laurence Roehm took his place, limiting U-M's offensive punch.

On second-and-7 from MAC's 27, Yost tried the same end-to-end pass, and it was open again. Lyons turned and wrapped his arms around the ball at the 8 yard line, and then the lightly regarded Hewitt Miller sprinted over, launched himself, and met Lyons with a crunching hit. In that split second the ball was jarred loose for an incompletion, and Hewitt Miller's name was cemented in MAC lore.

Two plays later, on fourth-and-7, Roehm dropped back for one last try, but Smith tore through the line and dropped him for a sack. All that remained for the Aggies was to run out the last few seconds on the clock—and enjoy each one of them.

No Letdown Here

Michigan State has had trouble over the years getting back up emotionally after Michigan games, but that was not a problem for the 1913 MAC Aggies. A week after scoring its first ever win over the Wolverines, MAC traveled to play Wisconsin, the defending Big Ten champ. "Wisconsin has a much more powerful team than the one MAC beat in Ann Arbor," wrote *Detroit Saturday Night.* "The student body had hardly recovered its sanity when the team went to Madison," remembered MAC's yearbook(strangely titled *The Wolverine* at the time).

But the Aggies claimed their second giant upset in as many weeks, 12-7, thanks to a blocked punt for a touchdown and another score from star end Blake Miller. "Now that the conference champions have gone down before 'the farmers,' perhaps the people of this state will realize that the college at East Lansing has about the strongest football eleven in the west," *Detroit Saturday Night* proclaimed.

MAC went on to its first unbeaten, untied season, 7-0. The school wouldn't see another until Biggie Munn's national championship teams of 1951 and 1952.

Enjoy them they did, and then they paraded around Ann Arbor to the disgust of the locals. To that point the Wolverines had paid little mind to the Aggies—Notre Dame and Big Ten foes like Chicago and Ohio State were what really mattered— but now MAC had their full attention.

"Speaking of Armageddons, that will be a real game—that 1914 U-M–MAC affair," wrote *Detroit Saturday Night.* "The fans are already snuffing the battle afar off."

The fans in East Lansing enjoyed the win nearly as much as the players and boosters had in Ann Arbor. MAC called off Mon-

Blake Miller and the Aggies followed up their win over Michigan with an upset victory at mighty Wisconsin.

MAC's 1913 Season:

October 4	MAC 26, Olivet 0
October 11	MAC 57, Alma 0
October 18	MAC 12, Michigan 7
October 25	MAC 12, Wisconsin 7
November 1	MAC 41, Akron 0
November 8	MAC 13, Mt. Union 7
November 15	MAC 19, South Dakota 7

day classes in favor of a bonfire at the capitol building. It was a fitting end to a party that had started on Saturday evening with several impromptu blazes. One fire leveled a small barn on campus, near where the student union stands today. The barn belonged to Addison Makepeace Brown, secretary of the State Board of Agriculture.

Brown's cow was originally feared to have died in the fire — but as reported a few days later by the *State Journal*, the creature was spared because she had been led to the train station to greet MAC's heroes. All was well in Aggie land.

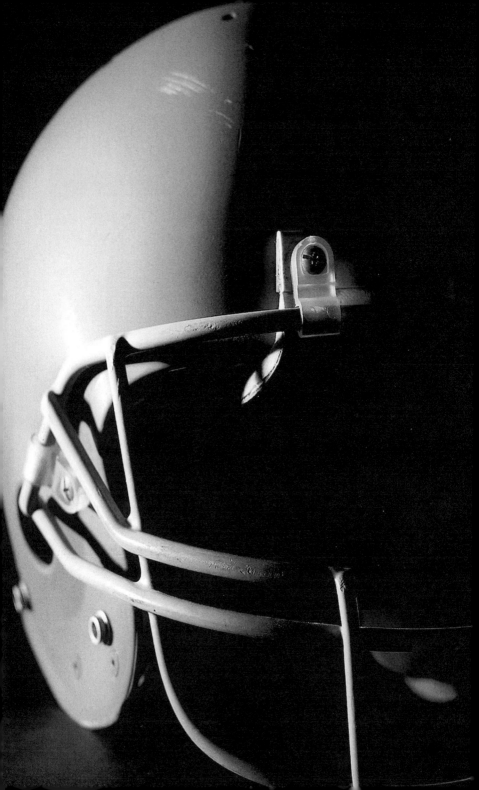

"It Can Get So Nasty"

Joseph Barrie stood outside Spartan Stadium, with the aid of a cane, squinting at a structure — with its 75,000 seats and luxury suites — that had changed immeasurably since he played there seventy years earlier. It was October 22, 2005, and Barrie, now ninety-four, was moments away from taking midfield as honorary captain of Michigan State's homecoming game with Northwestern. But he was thinking about a different game, one he'd never forget — that 16–0 victory over Michigan in 1934.

"What a day that was," remembered Barrie, at the time the lone surviving member of that 8–1 Michigan State College team. "We'd been waiting a long time to beat the Wolverines. And we beat them good."

The details were still vivid in Barrie's mind: his tangles in the middle of the line with Michigan center (and future U.S. president) Gerald Ford; MSC halfback Kurt Warmbein's two touchdown gallops; the pass-catching display put on by end Ed Klewicki; the euphoria Barrie shared with the cluster of Spartan fans who made the 63-mile trip to Ann Arbor. Along with teammates like Sid Wagner, Art Brandstatter, Don Wiseman, James McCrary, and Steve Sebo, Barrie had just been a part of the Spartans' third victory in twenty-nine tries against the Wolverines, and the first in nineteen years. "It was so big," Barrie said, "[Michigan State's] President Shaw declared a holiday and called off Monday's classes."

Such are the triumphant celebrations when Michigan State beats Michigan. They are wild and emotional, because they sure don't come every year. This has been a lopsided arrangement from the start. Michigan is college football's winningest program. It was playing the game and earning national attention for seventeen years before tiny Michigan Agricultural College even considered it. And in those early years, the Wolverines scoffed at the idea of a home-and-home series—thirty-six of the teams' first forty meetings took place in Ann Arbor.

More than one hundred years after the schools' first gridiron meeting (a 39–0 Michigan victory in 1898), the big brother–little brother relationship was intact. The Spartans have had stretches of dominance in this series and as a national program, but even in those times, wins over Michigan were cherished

This 1934 meeting with UM went to the Spartans, who were sporting striped helmets long before their rivals.

commodities. "We whipped 'em and we expected to whip 'em," declared Bob Apisa, a fullback on MSU's great teams of the late 1960s. "But it was still as big as anything. The 1966 'Game of the Century' with Notre Dame was huge, but for us the win over Michigan that season was still more important."

And Michigan? This is where the rivalry begins to turn bitter—when the Wolverines try to downplay it. Since the fierce, nationally televised battles between Woody Hayes's Ohio State and Bo Schembechler's Michigan in the 1970s, the nation has considered Michigan–Ohio State one of the game's greatest rivalries. Michigan and Notre Dame have had plenty of classic contests over the years and arguably boast more lore than anyone. But this much is clear: There's no one Michigan hates losing to more than those pesky Spartans.

"Michigan can say whatever they want. The fact is, Michigan's biggest rival is Michigan State," said Jim Hinesly, a senior left tackle on the 1978 MSU team that beat Michigan in Ann Arbor, snapping an eight-game losing streak in the series. "It's very simple. Most people from Michigan have to live with Michigan State people for their whole lives. They don't have to live with Ohio State people. And that's why this game means more, why it can get so nasty.

"You never want to use the term *hate*. But you're probably as close to that as you get when you line up for this game. There's nothing I've done in my life that's as intense as playing in that game. You could play it in the Meijer parking lot, and it would be just as intense."

That intensity was on display in 2004 and 2005, when the Wolverines pulled out overtime victories over the Spartans and celebrated wildly at midfield after each. Those were two of the series's greatest games, and there have been plenty: unranked MSU's 28–27 win over number one Michigan in Ann Arbor in 1990; Michigan's 10–7 win in East Lansing the season before, in which U-M safety Tripp Welborne stuffed MSU running back Blake Ezor on fourth-and-goal from the 1; the Spartans' 26–24 upset in 2001, on a Jeff Smoker–to–T.J. Duckett scoring toss with zeroes on the clock; MSU's 28–25 win in 1995, (Nick Saban's first year as MSU head coach) on a thrilling winning drive directed by quarterback Tony Banks; number seven Michigan's

17–10 comeback victory over number nine MSU in 1964, in which U-M scored two touchdowns in the final 6:42 to beat the Spartans for the first time since 1955; and the Wolverines' 1924 escape in a rare visit to East Lansing, when U-M needed a 45-yard Herb Steger catch-and-run with less than two minutes left to pull out a 7–0 win over coach Ralph Young's Aggies.

This series has also seen its share of blowouts. Michigan's 119–0 win in 1902, in the teams' second meeting, should stand forever as their most lopsided affair. The Wolverines also have wins of 63–0 (1922), 55–3 (1926), 55–0 (1947), 42–0 (1983), and 49–3 (2002) to their name. The Spartans counter with triumphs of 25–0 (1951), 35–6 (1957), 34–8 (1959), 28–0 (1961 and 1962), and 34–0 (1967).

Perhaps the most eye-popping green-and-white whipping came in 1915. Coach John F. Macklin's Aggies had scored MAC's first victory over U-M two seasons earlier, a 12–7 grinder. Quarterback Hub Huebel, who had played for Michigan in 1912, led the way to a 24–0 Aggies victory in Ann Arbor in 1915. MAC stars Gideon Smith, Blake Miller, Hewitt Miller, Jerry DaPrato, and Adelbert VanDervoort stood out in a complete demolition of Fielding Yost's Wolverines. Few in East Lansing could have suspected at the time that they would have to wait nineteen years for another triumph over the maize and blue.

In fact, from 1916 to 1932 MAC and MSC scored a total of one touchdown against the Wolverines. The Aggies (later Spartans) were shut out fifteen times. It got so bad, a 1926 Michigan State baseball win over Michigan actually inspired riots and fires in East Lansing.

That was the most dominating stretch for either program.

Clock Games

The name "Spartan Bob" will always be associated with the Michigan State–Michigan rivalry. It's the nickname of the Spartan Stadium clock keeper who, U-M fans claim, held the clock at one second when it should have run out in 2001. That extra tick allowed MSU quarterback Jeff

Smoker to drop back and loft a winning touchdown pass to running back T.J. Duckett. In the wake of MSU's 26–24 victory, U-M coach Lloyd Carr famously uttered the bitter words: "We deserved better." The clock operation in question was later analyzed by Big Ten officials and publicly deemed correct.

It wasn't the only game in this rivalry marred by controversial timekeeping. In 1910 the MAC Aggies were making a bid for their first victory over the Wolverines. Up 3–0, MAC thought it had the game clinched when halfback Leon "Bubbles" Hill scored on a long punt return. But a holding penalty wiped out the play. Michigan later scored on a disputed fake field goal to go up 6–3. With the Aggies trying to come back, Michigan's timekeeper said the game was over, even though MAC's

Jeff Smoker used the final tick to beat Michigan with this pass in 2001.

timekeeper claimed that about seven minutes remained on the clock. The officials went with Michigan's clock (there was no official game clock then), and the game was over.

While the Wolverines were flourishing under Yost, their East Lansing counterparts were struggling to find stability and a coach who could live up to Macklin's standards. But both sides have had their sustained moments. Michigan State finally found what it was looking for in coach Charlie Bachman, who arrived in 1933. That long-awaited win over Michigan in 1934 was the first of four straight over the Wolverines, by a combined score of 81–27. U-M was entering the worst stretch of its history, under coach Harry Kipke, a former Michigan football All-American who had coached MSC in 1928. "We were better than them," said Joe Barrie, who was a senior on the 1935 team that beat Michigan 25–6. "Charlie Bachman had us better prepared, and he had us believing that we were better."

The Spartans took complete control of the series in the 1950s and 1960s under Biggie Munn and then his protégé Duffy Daugherty. In those two decades, the Spartans went 14–4–2 against the Wolverines, taking charge of the state and becoming one of the nation's premier programs. That era of dominance was capped in 1969, when Daugherty's Spartans secretly switched during Michigan week from a veer option attack to the power-I. The move surprised U-M and its first-year coach, Bo Schembechler, and the Spartans ran away with a 23–12 win in East Lansing.

Schembechler would be back, though. And with the Daugherty era winding down—making way for a long stretch of instability at MSU—the Wolverines capitalized. From 1970 to 1983 Schembechler went 13–1 against the Spartans. The lone MSU bright spot was a 24–15 win in Ann Arbor in 1978, a game that coach Darryl Rogers's team, led by All-America receiver Kirk Gibson, controlled from start to finish.

Coach George Perles brought competitiveness back to the series in the 1980s. He arrived at MSU in 1983, got his first win over the Wolverines in 1984, and revived a rivalry that had been overshadowed by Michigan–Ohio State for the previous fifteen years. From 1984 to 2001 the Spartans took seven games from Michigan—four for Perles, two for successor Nick Saban, and one for Bobby Williams in 2001, the highlight of his short tenure in East Lansing.

Of course, those are just trends and statistics. It's the people involved who have made Michigan State–Michigan such a passionate annual affair. And many of them didn't wear helmets and shoulder pads. Perhaps the most contentious Spartan–Wolverine battle happened in the 1940s, when MSC was trying to gain entrance into the Big Ten. University president John Hannah, the man who turned Michigan State into a nationally prominent university, understood the role sports could play in such pursuits. He knew Big Ten membership would be a huge step toward legitimacy. Michigan knew it too, and its officials and coach Fritz Crisler made it their mission to keep Michigan State out.

"We knew from the beginning that there would be no friendly consideration of Michigan State's cause by the Big Ten if the University of Michigan had its way," Hannah wrote in his 1980 book, A Memoir. "We anticipated that Ann Arbor would be unfriendly and critical and obstructive, and that is exactly what they were, not only when we hoped to join the Big Ten, but later when we were being considered for membership in the American Association of Universities."

Ultimately, Michigan's objections were not enough. "Minnesota carried the torch for Michigan State," Hannah wrote.

"Purdue, Ohio State, Illinois, and Wisconsin supported us; the University of Michigan opposed us strenuously, and Indiana and Iowa were noncommittal. Northwestern, too, was friendly."

The Spartans were in, and Munn's team won the championship in its first year of Big Ten play, in 1953. Twenty years later, MSU got a chance to jab back at the Wolverines. Inbreeding is an element of any rivalry, and this one has its share of turncoats: Biggie Munn, a former assistant under Crisler at Michigan who went on to punish the Wolverines as the Spartans' head coach; Harry Kipke, a U-M player, then MSC coach, then U-M coach; Ralph Young, a standout player for Fielding Yost at U-M who went on to coach at Michigan State before serving as the Spartans' athletic director from 1923 to 1954; and Steve Stripling, who came to MSU as John L. Smith's defensive line coach in 2003, only to bail out for the same spot on U-M coach Lloyd Carr's staff in 2005. And then there was Burt Smith.

Smith, a U-M grad who played freshman football for the Wolverines, was part of MSU's athletic department in 1971 when Munn, then athletic director, suffered a stroke and had to retire. Smith took over on an interim basis and got the full-time job in 1972. And in November 1973 he faced an important decision. Michigan and Ohio State had just tied 10–10, and both had finished the season 10–0–1. The Big Ten's athletic directors were asked to submit a "secret" vote to determine whether the Wolverines or Buckeyes would go to the Rose Bowl. Smith voted against his alma mater; the Buckeyes prevailed by a single vote. News of Smith's vote got out. Schembechler raged for weeks to anyone who would listen. And in Ann Arbor Smith was permanently dubbed the traitor of all traitors.

Darryl Rogers became another of Ann Arbor's least favorites after his remarks at MSU's postseason banquet in 1978. Just weeks after the Spartans won 24–15 in Ann Arbor, Rogers referred to the Wolverines as "arrogant asses." The comment further endeared Rogers to his Spartan supporters and helped perpetuate the stereotypes that have driven this rivalry since its inception. U-M people, the Spartans say, are conceited elitists. MSU people, the Wolverines say, are country bumpkins. They were saying it in the late nineteenth century, and they were saying it in the early twenty-first century.

The typecasting was even mentioned in a 1956 *Time* magazine cover story on Duffy Daugherty: "All the offstage opposition mustered by MSU's Ann Arbor rival, the University of Michigan, could not keep it out of the Big Ten. In a league where almost every school is a symbol of state pride, the rivalry between Michigan and MSU became understandably bitter. This week the two rivals meet again, and Michigan's campus will be littered with signs reading CREAM MOO U, an unkind reference to State's beginnings as a cow college."

For as long as anyone can remember, the rivalry has been nasty on the field as well. Like other opponents, the Wolverines hurled racial slurs at MAC's black player, Gideon Smith, in the teams' 1913 game. In MSC's breakthrough 16–0 victory in 1934, star Kurt Warmbein offered a kick in the teeth to U-M center Gerald Ford after Ford clipped him. Trash talk was intense in the 1960s, and so was the hitting. MSU's George Webster hit Michigan end Jack Clancy so hard in the 1965 game, Clancy was knocked out, and Webster was Ann Arbor's newest villain. In 1984 Michigan quarterback Jim Harbaugh emerged from a pile of

George Webster (90) punished many Wolverines in MSU's 1965 win at Ann Arbor.

MSU bodies with a broken arm, and the Spartans went on to a 19–7 decision. In 2004 MSU was on its way to another upset in Ann Arbor before Michigan linebacker LaMarr Woodley grabbed MSU quarterback Drew Stanton and slammed him to the turf. The clean, punishing hit separated Stanton's shoulder and helped the Wolverines come back for a 45–37 overtime victory.

"It was real hard," Stanton said about watching his team let a 27–10 lead slip away late. "I can't even try to explain it." Those words are appropriate for anyone who tries to verbalize the inten-

The Greatest?

By 2004 a Michigan State–Michigan series that started in 1898 had produced plenty of worthy candidates to be considered the rivalry's best game. But the schools' ninety-seventh meeting just might be the new number one.

A chilly October 30 afternoon in Ann Arbor started with familiar expectations: number twelve U-M was expected to handle unranked MSU. But by midway through the second quarter, with the Spartans up 17–7, it was clear this game would be no easy hurdle for the Wolverines. MSU sophomore quarterback Drew Stanton was shredding the U-M defense, running second-year head coach John L. Smith's spread offense to perfection. Stanton had 95 yards passing and 80 yards rushing early, before he was knocked from the game in the second quarter on a hit by Michigan linebacker LaMarr Woodley.

The Spartans held strong, though, behind backup quarterback Damon Dowdell. Running back DeAndra Cobb's second long touchdown run made it 27–10 MSU with 8:43 left in the game, and the Spartans on the sideline reveled in their mammoth upset and arrival as a Big Ten contender.

"Of course we thought it was over," MSU linebacker Tyrell Dortch later told the *Lansing State Journal.* "I don't care if you're playing Oklahoma, if you're up 17 [that late] in the game, you think you've got it won."

But the Wolverines weren't done. A field goal, an onside kick, and two late touchdown passes to star wideout Braylon Edwards tied it up. The teams traded field goals, then touchdowns, in the first two extra sessions, before Edwards's third scoring grab gave his team a 45–37 victory in the third overtime. "It was one of the greatest football games I've ever been involved with, and I would have said that whether we won or lost," U-M coach Lloyd Carr said afterward.

On the MSU side, it was harder to immediately appreciate a contest that had thrilled the nation. "Any time you lose to your rival, it's the worst thing there is," Smith said. "I thought we were better and capable of winning."

sity and emotion that envelop one of college football's great rivalries. The partnership has not always been equal. But it has always been important for both sides. And when the Spartans score a triumph over the Wolverines, they savor it for a lifetime.

For ninety-four-year-old Joseph Barrie, the details of the Spartans' 16–0 victory over the Wolverines in 1934 were still crisp in his mind seventy-one years later. Details of the following Monday, with its impromptu class cancellations and parade, were not as clear. "I don't remember what I did," Barrie said. "I probably slept all day."

Birth of a Dynasty

It started as a trickle, then gradually gained force until the tiny visitor's locker room in Michigan Stadium was flooded with sewage. It didn't stop flowing until it was four inches deep—on a floor the Michigan State Spartans had abandoned moments before. They finished dressing while standing on the benches, balancing themselves carefully while trying to ignore the overpowering stench. Once their cleats were on, each man leaped off the bench and splashed toward the door and dry safety.

It was September 27, 1947, and just a few minutes before Clarence "Biggie" Munn's debut as Michigan State College's fourteenth head football coach. Munn was already tense that day in Ann Arbor. This had been his home for eight years as an assistant coach under Michigan great Fritz Crisler. Before that, Munn had been an assistant under Crisler at Minnesota, Munn's alma mater. Munn was the Big Ten's MVP in 1931 as a 200-pound lineman with the Golden Gophers, and he was a record-holder in several track events in Minnesota and the Big Ten. Coaching naturally followed an athletic career of such distinction. When Crisler and Munn arrived in Ann Arbor in 1938, the Wolverines had lost four straight games to Charlie Bachman's Spartans, prompting U-M to fire its coach, Harry Kipke. Crisler immediately turned that series around and returned the Wolverines to national prominence, and in 1946 Munn finally got a head coaching shot, at Syracuse.

In East Lansing a string of coaches tried but failed to duplicate the success John Macklin achieved in his short tenure (1911–15)—including Kipke, who was 3–4–1 in one season with the Spartans in 1928. Jim Crowley, famous as one of Notre Dame's Four Horsemen, showed up the next year and guided MSC (which had changed its name from Michigan Agricultural College in 1925) to four strong seasons. He went 22–8–3 but then packed up in 1933 for a chance to coach Fordham. Enter Bachman, a former teammate of Knute Rockne's at Notre Dame who would immediately endear himself to fans of MSC by beating Michigan in his second season. It was the Wolverines' first loss to the Spartans since 1915 and the first of four straight. Bachman went on to a 70–34–1 record in fourteen seasons, but by the

Biggie Munn was the Big Ten MVP in 1931 as a lineman for Minnesota.

end of his tenure it was clear that his program was going in the opposite direction of Crisler's. MSC president John Hannah sought a young, innovative coach who could bring the Spartans to new levels. He found Munn and lured him to East Lansing after just one season at Syracuse.

Seeing his protégé suddenly coaching a rival school in the same state did not sit well with Crisler. And the two men didn't have the closest of personal relationships in the first place. (Munn liked to refer to Crisler as "Kris Kringle.") Soon after Munn's hiring, he and Crisler were guests at the same banquet. They had not spoken since Munn's departure from Ann Arbor, and when Munn approached, Crisler famously greeted him with an icy scowl and these words: "And what are *you* doing back in the state of Michigan?" In case Munn wasn't sure before, he knew now: Crisler was going to try to embarrass him in the season opener in Ann Arbor.

When Munn began drilling his new team in the fall of 1947, the Spartans quickly realized they were dealing with a demanding perfectionist. They also sensed big things to come, thanks to Munn's imagination on offense and his talented staff of assistants: Hugh "Duffy" Daugherty, Forest Evashevski, and Kip Taylor. Bachman's "Flying Z" offense, a single wing attack with the backs lined up in a Z, had become gradually less effective over the years. "I knew we could get a lot better with a different offense," said Lynn Chandnois, a halfback who was one of Munn's first All-Americans. "Bachman was a good coach, but he was old school. The single wing we used was so dang old, we were the only college using it. There was no deception in it whatsoever. Either you ran right or you ran left."

The Munn Tree

Former Michigan State coach Biggie Munn and his successor, Duffy Daugherty, put together some of the best staffs in college football history. Here are some of the assistant coaches who worked for one or both of them in East Lansing:

- Bob Devaney (coached at MSU 1954–56): Became head coach at Nebraska and won two national championships.
- Dan Devine (1954): Had head coaching stints at Arizona State, at Missouri, with the Green Bay Packers, and with Notre Dame, where he won the national title in 1977.
- Earle Edwards (1949–53): Coached N.C. State 1954–70.
- Forest Evashevski (1947–49): Coached Iowa 1952–60.
- John McVay (1962–64): Became vice president/general manager of the San Francisco 49ers.
- George Perles (1967–71): Constructed Pittsburgh Steelers' "Steel Curtain" defense and was MSU's head coach 1983–94.
- Jimmy Raye (1971–75): Former MSU quarterback; has been an NFL assistant for twenty-nine years, including assistant head coach/offensive coordinator with the Oakland Raiders in 2004 and 2005.

Munn had all kinds of ideas about offense—ideas that would eventually revolutionize college football. He would soon begin installing an offense, the "Michigan State Multiple," in which the Spartans would start in a T formation and shift into a variety of

Biggie Munn compiled an astounding record of 54–9–2 in his seven seasons at MSU.

offensive sets, confounding defenses for years to come. But it would take some time for full installation and perfection, time Munn did not have before matching wits with his bitter mentor. In the short term, he had to keep things simple. MSC had three weeks to prepare for the Wolverines, who had returned the bulk of a team that finished the 1946 season ranked number six. Halfbacks Bob Chappuis and Bump Elliott led a team that, the Spartans learned later, had been given this edict from Crisler regarding MSC: "No mercy." Munn, meanwhile, immediately had the respect of his players and had them believing they could compete with Michigan.

The Spartans were fired up for the annual trip to Ann Arbor (the game had not been played in East Lansing since 1924), and by the time they got to the sideline, sewage dripping off their legs and shoes, they were frenzied. Told of the locker room disaster, Michigan officials shrugged and said a pipe must have cracked. "We didn't think it was accidental, let's put it that way," said George Guerre, a star halfback from 1946 to 1948.

The Spartans also wouldn't think it was the worst thing that happened to them that day, by the time the day was done. Crisler's squad, which would go on to a 10–0 season and national championship, unloaded on Munn's overmatched players. U-M kept piling it on until the scoreboard read 55–0, the most lopsided Wolverine win in the series in twenty-five years. Munn was humbled, so much so that he had a difficult time walking into his team's putrid quarters. "I almost broke into tears," Munn said later. "I could hardly bring myself to go into the locker room and face my boys."

Players who were there say tears were streaming when Munn said this: "I've been humiliated. We've all been humiliated. But if you're the kind of guys I think you are, we'll come back and have our day."

Munn's debut at Macklin Field brightened everyone's outlook considerably. The Spartans battled for a 7–0 win over a tough Mississippi State team. Wins over Washington State and Iowa State followed. Next was a visit from Kentucky, led by coach Paul "Bear" Bryant and quarterback George Blanda. The Wildcats led 7–0 late when Guerre, a smallish speedster nicknamed "Little Dynamite," ripped off a 75-yard run to the Kentucky 10. On the next play, he weaved his way into the end zone but in the process took a hit that broke his leg. The Spartans then missed the extra point. Munn, having seen his team lose one of its stars and an important game in bang-bang succession, was crestfallen.

He was so down, in fact, that he seriously considered hanging it up the next week. A Guerre appearance at a prep banquet in Flint changed his mind. "I give George Guerre credit for keeping me in coaching," Munn told *Sports Illustrated* in a 1962 interview. "I was rather discouraged and just about ready to quit football entirely. . . . [At the banquet] somebody asked him in a rather sarcastic way, 'What kind of guy is this Biggie Munn anyway?' Well sir, George looked the fellow right in the eye and said, 'Biggie Munn is the kind of a guy you're glad to break a leg for.' Well, I said to myself, if a coach can win this kind of respect from players, I'm staying with this game."

Rejuvenated after hearing of Guerre's remarks, Munn led the Spartans to victories in their final four games to finish 7–2. Confidence was restored, and recruiting momentum was picking up, especially with Michigan State's imminent entry into the Big Ten. Crisler and Michigan had been fighting hard to keep the

Spartans out, but MSC president Hannah had the votes, and MSU was admitted to the Big Ten in December 1948 (although the football team wouldn't start competing in the league until 1953 because of advance scheduling). On the field, Munn's vision was starting to take hold with his players. His famous line was, "The difference between good and great is a little extra effort," and he certainly extracted maximum intensity from his players. But that was just part of the reason he was able to build Michigan State into a national football power.

In the late forties, college football players got bigger and stronger every year, it seemed. Munn opted to go the other way, as illustrated by this line from his book *Michigan State Multiple Offense*: "Sacrifice everything for speed and quickness. They are the keys to success in modern football." Munn sought smaller, faster linemen who could execute his plays on offense and swarm to the ball on defense. Until he could fill his roster with his own players, Munn also displayed something rare in coaches: flexibility. "That was the thing about Biggie that made him special," Guerre says. "He'd develop his plays and his system around the talent he had. Most coaches had their system, and that was it."

When Munn got his own players, things really started to take off. He found smaller, unheralded athletes at tiny Michigan high schools, such as Billy Wells of Menominee, Gordie Serr of Corunna, Rex Corless of Coldwater, and Al Dorow of Imlay City. He landed future stars in halfbacks LeRoy Bolden and Don McAuliffe, guards Don Mason and Frank Kush, and quarterbacks Tom Yewcic and Earl Morrall. He scored arguably his biggest recruiting victory in 1948, when he landed Flint Central tackle Don Coleman. Munn's assistant and line coach, Duffy

LeRoy Bolden (right) was an All-America halfback in Munn's final season of 1953.

Daugherty, made the difference—as was often the case on the recruiting trail. Coleman picked MSC over Michigan and several other Big Ten offers and ultimately developed into one of the best players in the school's history.

"I'll never forget what Duffy said to me: 'Don, we need you,'" Coleman remembered. "That clinched it for me." At 5'11", 175 pounds, Coleman was undersized for a major college tackle. And his rapid metabolism wouldn't allow him to put on any weight. (Munn, like most coaches at the time, shunned the idea of weight lifting.) Coleman had to sit out his freshman year, as required, but once he got onto the field as a sophomore, Munn knew he had a special talent. Coleman was wiry-strong and fast, able to shed blocks and chase ballcarriers all over the field on defense and take out multiple defenders in a single play on offense. At times Coleman would actually seal a defender in the hole, allowing his back to run through, and then race downfield, catch up with the weaving runner, and lead the way for more yardage. Often he would take out two or three men at the point of attack. Guards Don Mason and Ed Bagdon helped him form a line known as "Duffy's Toughies," and Munn took their quick feet into account as he perfected his system.

And what a system it was. To opponents it appeared outrageously complex. The Spartans would usually start in a T formation, then shift before the snap into any number of offensive looks: the split T, single wing, double wing, winged T. Munn would run some plays out of a short-punt look, and he even toyed with something that at the time was called a spread. (It was actually just the split T, with the ends spread out a little farther than normal.) The genius of Munn's system was that his playbook was

A New Standard

Biggie Munn had no idea what could be expected of an offensive lineman until he saw Don Coleman play. "It's not unusual to see Don take out two or three men on a single play," Munn once said of Coleman, a tackle from Flint who also starred on the defensive side of the ball. Coleman also played on every special-teams unit, earning himself the title "sixty-minute man."

Coleman was so effective on offense, Munn began drawing up plays that required his offensive tackles to complete more than one block. It was a lofty standard for those who followed Coleman. At 5'11", 175 pounds, he was believed to be the smallest tackle in major college football. He was also known as one of the toughest.

Coleman shunned face masks, which were optional but were growing in popularity. As an All-America senior in 1951, Coleman had his nose ripped in a victory over Penn State, a wound that required twelve stitches. Michigan State's trainers wouldn't let him return to the game until they had fashioned a protective bar onto the helmet. Despite the injury and the obstruction, Coleman had what he called "my greatest game," making every tackle on MSU's kickoffs and punts.

Months after Coleman's career was finished, Munn retired his number 78 jersey. It was the first of only three jerseys retired in Michigan State's history.

"I'm very proud of that honor," said Coleman. "But I'm more proud of the fact that I became the first black coach at Michigan State." Coleman joined Duffy Daugherty's staff for one season, in 1968. He then went on to a long career as an MSU faculty member, mostly in the department of osteopathic medicine.

actually confined mostly to a dozen or so bread-and-butter plays. But the mass of formations had heads spinning. "I don't see how a college team can be taught so much offense," wrote the *Portland Oregonian* in 1948, after Munn's team smashed Oregon State 46–21. "Even the pros don't do it."

Michigan State's first three offensive plays of each game were scripted beforehand. Each week Munn would install four or five new plays, devised especially for the opponent at hand. But he wouldn't just install them. "You'd run them in practice until you slept with them," Guerre recalled. "You'd dream about them."

Munn's attention to detail was legendary. Half of each practice was devoted strictly to fundamentals and the other half to carrying out each play, each assignment, with utter precision. Using a stopwatch, Munn would demand exactness down to tenths of seconds—and he'd practice a play as many times as necessary until he got it. The deception of Munn's offense would go only so far if it wasn't carried out perfectly. At times that required Munn to get tough.

As a senior All-American, Lynn Chandnois once disagreed with Munn's contention that he was running a play wrong in practice. Munn took the opportunity to send a message. "Don't you talk back to me, ever!" Munn screamed. "Or I'll give you hell like you wouldn't believe." Message received: No one was above reproach. And that included assistant coaches. Daugherty often softened Munn's demanding ways with a gentle hand, providing a good cop–bad cop symmetry. "Biggie was a stern disciplinarian, and we appreciated that," Coleman explained. "Duffy was a warm, gregarious person who got the best out of you in a smooth, silky kind of way."

At times Daugherty would let his linemen take quick breathers during grueling practices when the team split into positional drills. He'd usually tell them a joke to lift their spirits, and on one occasion a punch line elicited loud laughter from his audience. Munn, perched as he often was in a tower overlooking the practice field, scowled and picked up his bullhorn. "Duffy! Duffy! Get those bums to work!" Munn screamed. "This is no laughing matter!"

That's not to say Munn was humorless. He actually enjoyed joking with, and playing pranks on, his players—off the practice field. And he tried to be creative as a motivator. At halftime of one game against an inferior foe, the Spartans entered the locker room tied. Munn emerged after a few moments holding a briefcase. "The trouble with you guys," Munn said, "is that you read too darn many of your press clippings!" He opened the briefcase, dumped a season's worth of newspaper articles about the Spartans onto the floor, and stormed out. Lineman Pete Fusi, the team jokester, walked over to the pile of papers, picked one up, and started reading. The Spartans went out and dominated the second half.

MSU expanded the capacity of Macklin Field from 26,000 to 51,000 before the 1948 season, and Michigan was scheduled to show up for the opener. It was U-M's first visit to East Lansing in twenty-four years. The Spartans had adapted to Munn's style and system in one year, and "we got a hell of a lot better," Chandnois said. It showed. The Wolverines—coached now by Bennie Oosterbaan, after Crisler's off-season retirement—needed a touchdown late in the fourth quarter to escape 13–7. The Spartans had made up 49 points in the span of a year. And with official Big Ten

Rosy Reward

Michigan State's 6-0 upset loss to Purdue in 1953 stopped an incredible twenty-eight-game winning streak for the Spartans, and it also forced Michigan State to share the Big Ten championship with Illinois—in MSC's first year in the league.

When the Big Ten conference athletic directors voted for MSC over Illinois as the league's representative in the Rose Bowl, the announcement brought unprecedented celebration in the Lansing area. A contingent of 15,000 Spartan fans headed west. The *Lansing State Journal*'s Seth Whitmore traveled with one of the large motorcades and filed daily stories from Route 66.

The Spartans saw plenty of action in Los Angeles before game day. Halfback Billy Wells got to take Debbie Reynolds on a date. MSC's Bill Quinlan and Henry Bullough happened upon a hotel fire and carried a woman to safety, then joined with teammates to control the blaze until firefighters arrived.

When the game finally started, the Spartans fell behind 14-0 to the underdog UCLA Bruins. That should not have come as a surprise to Spartan fans—in coach Biggie Munn's final thirty-three games, the Spartans had won thirty-two, but they had to come from behind in fourteen of them. End Ellis Duckett's blocked punt and return for a touchdown turned the game around for MSC, and the Spartans went on to win 28-20. Wells, who returned a punt 62 yards for a touchdown, was named the game's MVP.

After going 54-9-2 in seven years as Michigan State's coach, Munn retired after the game to become the school's athletic director. He served in that role for eighteen years before suffering a pair of strokes and dying in Lansing in 1975, at age sixty-six.

Biggie got a lift out of this 1950 upset win over Notre Dame.

membership just a couple months away, it was easy to see where the Spartans were headed.

In 1949 the Spartans edged closer to U-M, losing 7–3, en route to a 6–3 season. In 1950 Munn finally broke through with a 14–7 win over the Wolverines in Ann Arbor, led by All-America halfback Sonny Grandelius. The next week MSC lost 34–7 to Maryland, which was running a strange new system some were calling the "option." It was a big disappointment. It was also the last time the Spartans would lose for more than three years.

Twenty-eight victories in a row. Munn's offense, his recruiting tactics, his motivational expertise, and his school's rapid growth came together to form a college football giant. In 1950 MSC appeared on TV and finished in the national top ten for the first time. In 1951, Coleman's senior year, MSU went 9–0 and finished number two in the polls to Tennessee. In 1952 McAuliffe, Yewcic, Kush, Bolden, James Ellis, Ellis Duckett, Don Dohoney, Larry Fowler, Dick Tamburo, and company ran the table again, and this time MSC was voted national champion in the AP and UPI polls. In 1953 the Spartans began Big Ten play and took the league in their first try. Munn scored his fourth straight win over the suddenly secondary Wolverines.

An upset loss at Purdue on October 24, 1953, halted the winning streak, but Michigan State finished the season by beating UCLA 28–20 in the Rose Bowl. The victory was celebrated as the greatest athletic achievement in MSC's history. Munn had come a long way from standing in sewage in the bowels of Michigan Stadium, and he showed his usual impeccable timing, leaving coaching right after the game to become MSC's athletic director.

When his stunning seven-year run was over, Munn had a record of 54–9–2. That's a winning percentage of .857—a mark that compares favorably with some of the most celebrated runs in coaching, including Crisler's .816 at Michigan and Ara Parseghian's .817 at Notre Dame. And to think he almost quit after a few weeks, before a player's supportive words swayed him to stay.

"He was tough on us, but we all loved him because we knew he cared for us," Coleman said. "And we didn't just love him—we stood in awe of him."

Teams Beyond Their Times

Charles "Bubba" Smith knew what it meant, even if most of his teammates had no idea. The moment Michigan State coach Hugh "Duffy" Daugherty named his starting defense before the 1965 season, Smith knew that this team could afford nothing but greatness.

Daugherty called out eleven names in that meeting, with eleven corresponding positions.

They included Harold Lucas, defensive tackle; Jess Phillips, safety; Bubba Smith, defensive end; Jim Summers, defensive back; Charlie Thornhill, linebacker; George Webster, roverback. Six African Americans on one starting defense, at a time when southern programs were all white, and most other programs had no more than a handful of minorities on their entire rosters. Six African Americans on one starting defense, joining four black starters on MSU's offense—and setting Daugherty's program up to either reject or reinforce racist views that were still disturbingly common at the time.

"I knew that was something that had never happened before," Smith recalled. "I went to each man individually. I said, 'This is our chance. We've got to do this. If we don't do this, it will never happen again.' We had to show that we could be leaders, and winners."

And so did Daugherty. Consider his position at the time: Since taking over for mentor Clarence "Biggie" Munn in 1954, Daugherty had endured a successful but occasionally rocky existence at MSU. He and Munn had gotten into a well-publicized shouting match in MSU president John Hannah's office after Daugherty's first season, a 3–6 disappointment. Daugherty responded by winning the 1956 Rose Bowl and a claim to the national championship. The Spartans got another piece of the national title in 1957, but Daugherty also had two more losing seasons with a program that had done nothing but win under Munn. When Daugherty's talented 1964 team struggled to a 4–5 record, he came under heavy criticism. And now he was going into the next season with a lineup that, frankly, was bound to make some people feel uncomfortable.

Bubba Smith dominated at defensive end for MSU—and he knew well the social impact of MSU's 1965 defensive team.

For Daugherty, it was simply about getting his best players onto the field. But there was an unwritten rule in college football at the time concerning African Americans: Don't recruit too many, and don't play too many, or risk losing alumni money and fan support. "You just didn't do it," said Clinton Jones, the star halfback in 1965 and 1966. MSU's football program had long been considered socially progressive, going back to the 1910s with tackle Gideon Smith, one of the first black college and pro football players, and continuing into the Munn era with stars such as Don Coleman, James Ellis, LeRoy Bolden, and Ellis Duckett. Sherman Lewis and Earl Lattimer were among the African American standouts of Daugherty's first ten years. There was pride in that reputation, but this 1965 lineup went a step or two beyond what anyone else had attempted.

"From what I heard, he did take a lot of guff for it," remembered Charlie Thornhill. "Duffy took a chance. And that's why I appreciate what he did for me and the other black players. Duffy wanted to be the first one to take that giant step. Times were changing then, but Duffy was ahead. But it wasn't just that. The thing about Duffy is, he treated us all the same way because he cared for us all the same."

Thornhill, a star running back from Roanoke, Virginia, was about to commit to play for Notre Dame in 1963 when he met Alabama coach Paul "Bear" Bryant at a banquet in his hometown. Bryant took Thornhill aside and talked about his future, assuring him that, soon enough, southern schools would start opening their doors to African American athletes. Bryant helped sway Thornhill away from Notre Dame and toward MSU—as he did with many players over the years for Daugherty, one of his

Miner to Major

Hugh "Duffy" Daugherty was twenty-two, working in a coal mine in western Pennsylvania just like his father had, when he got the break of his life. A coach for Syracuse had noticed Daugherty playing offensive line in a semipro game and offered him a scholarship. Daugherty jumped at the chance. At Syracuse he played for a line coach named Clarence "Biggie" Munn. Daugherty broke his neck early in his career, but he came back to play well and captain the team during his senior year.

After serving in World War II and ascending to the rank of major, Daugherty came back to Syracuse, where Munn was now head coach. Daugherty became Munn's line coach in 1946, and the pair moved to East Lansing the next year, when Munn got the Michigan State coaching job. Daugherty earned $3,500 a year to coach MSU's line. Munn moved upstairs to athletic director after seven incredibly successful years (54-9-2), leaving Daugherty with the unenviable task of maintaining his standards—amid public criticism at times from Munn. Daugherty survived to go 109-69-5 in nineteen years, retiring as MSU's winningest coach.

Duffy Daugherty became the face of MSU football.

He earned MSU a claim to four national championships (1955, 1957, 1965, and 1966); won a pair of Big Ten titles; beat UCLA in the 1956 Rose Bowl; achieved seven finishes in the national top ten; went 10-7-2 against Michigan and 10-7-1 against Notre Dame; tutored thirty-three first-team All-Americans; and came to be known as one of the most socially progressive coaches in college football, freely recruiting and playing African Americans at a time when many did not.

close friends in the profession. In the same year, Daugherty got Bubba Smith and blazing-fast end Gene Washington from Texas. He plucked George Webster, destined to become perhaps MSU's best player ever, from South Carolina. Coast to coast, Daugherty recruited the best players he could find, disregarding color, and the result was a roster with fifteen African Americans on his 1965 team and sixteen on his 1966 team.

With so many players from the South witnessing integrated society for the first time, major culture shock was inevitable. Smith had never so much as spoken to a white person before he arrived in East Lansing. Webster had some white friends as a young child, but they stayed separate once they reached their teens. Thornhill had his mind made up about white people before he ever came to town. It didn't help when his scheduled dormitory roommate walked in with his parents, saw Thornhill, and walked right back out. The parents complained and got their son a white roommate.

"My freshman year I got into a lot of altercations with people. White people," Thornhill stated. "Coming from the South, I had a chip on my shoulder. My peers told me 'You can't trust white people,' and I took that to heart. When you're sitting in a class with two hundred kids, and you're the only black, it's a shock. But I got over it."

Clinton Jones had gone to an all-white Catholic school in Cleveland—where his teammates gave him the nickname "Uncle Tom"—and at MSU he was almost immediately thrust into the role of counsel for many of his homesick teammates. "It seems like every week I was talking somebody out of leaving," he remembered. While the southerners acclimated themselves to

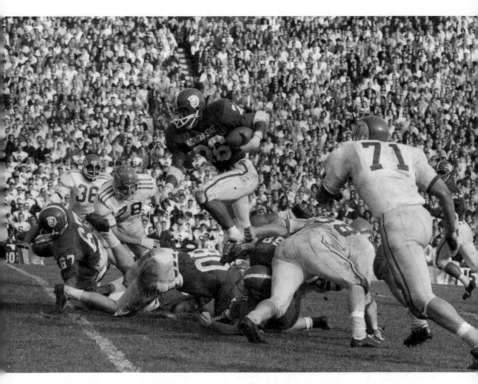

Clinton Jones was a star runner who also helped bridge the racial divide between black and white players.

midwestern life, many of the white, rural midwesterners were adjusting as well. Daugherty insisted, emphatically when necessary, that his white and black players eat together, room together, hang out together, and make a genuine effort to know one another. The world outside MSU's campus was rife with social unrest, race riots, and a civil rights movement in full swing. Many Spartans were insulated from such concerns, until teammates such as Thornhill and Smith told them about their lives.

"To me, it was shocking to hear about separate eating, separate bathrooms, riding in the back of the bus," said Don Japinga, a senior defensive back and co-captain on the 1965 team who hailed from tiny, all-white Wayland, Michigan. "Those guys would tell us about all these things, and we'd really start to understand where they were coming from. The closeness on our team, [for] everyone, became very, very strong."

All this bonding didn't help the 1964 team win games. But with some position switches (most notably, Daugherty moved Webster from defensive end to roverback) and personnel moves (after keeping Smith in the doghouse for long stretches of the 1964 campaign, the coach made him a full-time starter in 1965), Daugherty felt like he had a winner with his 1965 team. He had a talented senior quarterback, Steve Juday. Jones and Washington were primed for big things as juniors, after getting their feet wet as sophomores (freshmen were ineligible at the time). Sophomore fullback Bob Apisa, from Hawaii, was fleet and powerful. The offensive line was strong, led by All-America tackle Jerry West. And the defense had discovered Thornhill midway through the 1964 season, after Daugherty tried him at linebacker on a whim during one practice. Thornhill, who had been working as a scout team fullback, was so dominant, so completely unblockable, Daugherty told defensive coordinator Hank Bullough to start him the next week at Wisconsin. He was a mainstay from then on. Ron Goovert was equally forceful as a senior linebacker in 1965. The line was powerful, manned by massive Harold Lucas inside and bolstered tremendously by Smith's permanent, 6'7", 290-pound presence. Jess Phillips was a huge hitter and Japinga a ballhawk. Taken together, they were a brash, nasty group. Trash talk was part of the game for this team. Practices saw regular fistfights between the starters and the scout team.

"We had a lot of intense—extremely intense—individuals who didn't want to lose," Japinga said. "And they definitely didn't want to get shown up by the people we were playing against. People have asked me a lot how we could get up for every game. My response is, we got up for every practice."

The 1965 season would require maximum motivation from the start, with nonleague games scheduled against UCLA and Penn State, followed in order by Big Ten powers Illinois, Michigan, Ohio State, and Purdue. The new-look defense immediately established itself as formidable in the opener, a 13–3 suffocation of the Bruins at Spartan Stadium. It was downright impenetrable the next week at State College, Pennsylvania, in a 23–0 romp. The Nittany Lions' best chance at points came on a kickoff return by halfback Mike Irwin—who was caught from behind by Bubba Smith. In the Big Ten opener, the Spartans faltered a bit before coming back to beat Illinois 22–12, avenging a 16–0 loss the season before.

Juday was on his way to breaking several school passing records, and his favorite target, Washington, was doing the same with the receiving records. Jones and Apisa were forming into an All-America backfield, with quality help from halfback Dwight Lee and fullback Eddie Cotton. But it was the defense that was opening eyes, and the swarming Spartans were just getting started. Up next was defending Big Ten and Rose Bowl champ Michigan, which had delivered the most disheartening loss of MSU's 1964 season—scoring a pair of touchdowns in the final six minutes, the latter on a halfback option pass, to come back for a

17–10 win. It was Michigan's first win in the series since 1955.

Webster had been obliterating ballcarriers all over the field from his new roverback position and gaining some notice for it, but it was the Michigan game that established him as a national name. He stopped the Wolverines all by himself on five straight plays to start the second half, knocked Michigan end Jim Clancy from the game with a head-on shot after a short pass to Clancy, and added an interception and a fumble recovery. The Wolverines ran for minus-39 yards, and Apisa galloped 39 positive yards on the final play of the game for an in-your-face touchdown and final margin of 24–7.

The word was out: This was a great team with a potentially legendary defense. Ohio State found that out the next week, going for minus-22 yards on the ground. Woody Hayes's famed "three yards and a cloud of dust" offense did not get a first down rushing. And the Buckeyes did not have one rushing attempt in the second half, opting instead to try twenty-nine straight passes. The Spartans rolled 32–7, and Hayes was so steamed he refused to shake Clinton Jones's hand after the game. Jones, a native of Cleveland, had been recruited by Hayes but had chosen Daugherty and the Spartans instead, earning an angry hang-up from Hayes when he gave him the news. Apparently the bitterness had not dissipated.

With Michigan and Ohio State dispatched, the Spartans faced one remaining serious obstacle before they could claim the Big Ten championship. Purdue and quarterback Bob Griese were waiting for MSU in West Lafayette, Indiana. MSU had shot up to number two in the polls, and the Boilermakers, 4–0–1 overall and 2–0 in the Big Ten, were number six. Griese was sharp early, throwing a touchdown, then kicking the extra point and adding a field goal for a score of Griese 10, MSU 0 at halftime. But Webster, Smith, and the Spartans started getting to him in the second half, and the Boilermakers offense was done. Jones scored twice in the second half, and MSU survived, 14–10.

Subsequent blowouts of Northwestern, Iowa, and Indiana got the Spartans their league title, Rose Bowl bid, and number one ranking. A 12–3 win at number four Notre Dame to end the regular season—another national showcase for Webster and the defense, which held the Fighting Irish to minus-12 rushing and 24 passing, for a grand total of a dozen yards—clinched MSU's first national championship since 1957. Until that season, neither of the major polls recognized bowl results. The United Press International poll remained that way in 1965 and closed with MSU on top. But for the first time, the Associated Press poll waited to make its rankings until the bowl games were finished. That mattered little to the Spartans, who were getting a rematch with UCLA in the Rose Bowl and expected to blow out the Bruins again.

In fact, everyone expected the Spartans to blow out the Bruins, and both teams apparently were reading all about it. MSU's lack of focus concerned Daugherty so much, he moved the team away from the nightlife of Los Angeles and into a secluded monastery for the last couple of days before the game, but that only seemed to anger his players. "It was a short prison sentence," Apisa said later. On game day the Bruins scored after Japinga fumbled a punt deep in his own end; then they recovered a surprise onside kick and scored again on a short field for a 14–0 lead. The Spartans strangled UCLA's offense from there and got back

A Line for Every Occasion

MSU coach Duffy Daugherty had so many jokes stored up, he told his team a new one after each practice. Daugherty was a favorite among reporters and on the banquet circuit for his witty one-liners. Among the most famous:

- "I could have been a Rhodes Scholar, except for my grades."
- "We're small, but we're slow."
- "I like those goal-line stands of ours, but I wish they'd make them up around the 50 yard line where I can see them better."
- On mentor Biggie Munn's College Football Hall of Fame induction: "You can credit me for getting Biggie into the Hall of Fame. After six years of my coaching, they appreciate what a great coach he really was."
- At an MSU football banquet: "Look at our Bubba Smith, he used to be an 89-pound weakling—when he was three years old."
- Asked whom he was most happy to see back for the 1965 season: "Me!"
- After accidentally spilling his coffee on a playbook in front of reporters: "Oh well, we have to learn to play on a wet field anyway."
- On the 1967 team's 3–7 record: "We won three games, lost none, and were upset in seven."

into it in the second half with a 38-yard touchdown run by Apisa, followed by a failed 2-point conversion. Juday snuck it in to cut the UCLA lead to 14–12, but then Apisa was stopped just shy of the goal line on the 2-point conversion try.

The loss, which Daugherty later said was the biggest regret of his career, forced MSU to share the national title with Alabama. It would also be the only defeat MSU would suffer in 1965 and 1966. "We were not enthused about the game," Apisa recalled. "We were young guys, and we thought we were hot crap. We said, 'Well, we mopped these guys up before, and we're gonna do it again.' . . . If we played UCLA ten times, nine times we would have waxed them. And they've even admitted that."

Despite the somber finish, the Spartans were greeted as heroes upon their return home. The 1965 season had been one of the best in school history, with likely the most talented team to wear the green and white. Bubba Smith's pleas to his African-American teammates to make this opportunity count had been answered resoundingly. And on and around campus, they were treated like movie stars. Smith, in particular, was a popular figure because of his tremendous size and outgoing personality. He regularly ventured outside of the football social circle and even joined a Jewish fraternity "to see what it was like." It took a while, but Thornhill had settled in as well and made some white friends. As for his short-term roommate—the one whose parents refused to let their son live with a black man—that young man was harassed by other students in the dorm once they heard the story, and he eventually had to move to another building. MSU's African-American players from that era still marvel at the way they were embraced, considering the time. "MSU was the one place that showed diversity, humanism, and respect toward one another that you didn't see on other campuses," Jones said.

For all the harmony set against racial strife elsewhere, there were reminders that all was not equal. MSU's black players were prohibited from dating white women (a rule that Smith, for one, openly violated before Daugherty quietly eased it), and at times it felt as if many of the regulations were a bit tighter for them than for their white counterparts. "There was no racial tension while I was there, but . . . we knew our place," Jones said. Racist comments occasionally reached the MSU bench in hostile stadiums, and jokes about Daugherty and his team made the rounds. Smith came across an article in a southern newspaper that referred to "Duffy feeding his monkeys bananas." And Daugherty himself took some heat locally despite his team's tremendous success. Some of his players thought alumni pressure was a factor when he started a white player in place of defensive back Jim Summers for a game in 1966.

Whether or not that was true, Daugherty did not step back in the larger sense. In fact, his 1966 team featured twelve black players among the starting twenty-two, including quarterback Jimmy Raye. And Jones and Webster were his captains. African Americans filled all of MSU's key leadership positions. If the 1965 team was a statement, the 1966 version was a public demonstration, amplified by the "Game of the Century" between number one Notre Dame and number two MSU to wrap up the season. That 10–10 tie, played out before a record 33 million viewers, justified Daugherty's vision and did inestimable good for the game's future.

That 1966 team also might have been better than the 1965

Father Knows Best

Charles "Bubba" Smith did not want to go to Michigan State. He would have liked to play for Darrell Royal at Texas, but that school's program was not yet integrated. He had his heart set on UCLA after receiving a call from Mel Farr, a friend and fellow native of Beaumont, Texas, who played for the Bruins. "He said, 'Hey man, I'm out on Bing Crosby's yacht,'" Smith later remembered. "'Get out here.'"

But Smith's father, a high school football coach in Beaumont, had formed a friendship with MSU coach Duffy Daugherty. And so he sent his son to East Lansing, despite the fact that Bubba and Duffy had never spoken. That was a recipe for trouble, and Bubba soon found himself in Duffy's doghouse. At 6'7", 290 pounds and with great speed, Smith was a defensive end unlike any other. But Daugherty sat him for much of his sophomore year. "I guess he was trying to control me," said Smith, who was never afraid to openly criticize Daugherty's coaching moves.

The two finally came to terms before the 1965 season, and Smith dominated games as a junior and senior. He also learned to love his new home, despite the rough winter weather, and he became a tremendously popular figure around campus. "It was the greatest time of my life," said Smith, who is still one of the greatest players to wear an MSU uniform—and the only one to be a number one overall pick in the NFL draft.

End Gene Washington made acrobatic plays like this routine at MSU.

lineup, despite heavy personnel losses. Webster, Smith, Thornhill, and company were even more dominating as seniors; same
for Jones and Washington on the offensive side. Raye took over
for Juday and provided the season's key moment. In driving rain
at Ohio State, he engineered a sixteen-play, 84-yard scoring drive
in the fourth quarter, completing four huge passes. Apisa finally
burst in for the decisive touchdown and 11–8 victory—which
kept the unbeaten season alive but allowed the Fighting Irish to

leapfrog the Spartans into the number one position in both polls. MSU was dominant otherwise, pounding Penn State and first-year coach Joe Paterno, 42–8; handling Michigan, 20–7; destroying Bob Griese and Purdue, 41–20; and warming up for Notre Dame with a combined score of 103–26 against Northwestern, Iowa, and Indiana. The season-ending tie ultimately allowed the Fighting Irish to finish atop both polls, although four independent selectors, including the National Football Foundation, picked MSU as national champ.

That Notre Dame game, as it turned out, was also the unofficial end of the Spartan football dynasty. The success of Daugherty's bold move ensured that many would copy it, and southern schools soon opened their doors to black athletes. But Daugherty had become MSU's all-time winningest coach and cemented himself as one of the game's legends with two teams that went 19–1–1 — and did so much more.

"We were the children of destiny, so to speak," said Clinton Jones. "You know, somebody should make a movie about those teams."

The Hit Maker

Michigan hands off to Dave Fisher. George Webster stops him for a gain of 1. Michigan throws to Jim Clancy. George Webster races to the sideline to knock him out of bounds after a gain of 10. Michigan throws to Steve Smith. George Webster pops him immediately, knocking the ball loose for an incompletion. Michigan runs Carl Ward. George Webster shoots into the backfield and wraps him up for a loss of 2. Michigan tries a screen pass to Ward. George Webster chases him down from behind after a gain of 7, forcing a punt.

Those five consecutive plays, to start the third quarter of the Michigan–Michigan State game on October 9, 1965, were some of the best the Wolverines came up with that day. They also introduced junior roverback George "Mickey" Webster to the nation. Left, right, up the middle, deep in the backfield, and far downfield—wherever the Michigan Wolverines went, Webster joined them. For all the reasons to revel in MSU's 24–7 smothering of the Wolverines, Webster's dominance of the action dominated the postgame discussion. "That George Webster had a heck of a game out there, didn't he?" MSU coach Duffy Daugherty said wryly after it was over.

MSU's overwhelming defense held Michigan to minus-39 yards rushing that day. Webster added an interception, a fumble recovery, and a jarring hit on Clancy that knocked the Wolverine out of the game and earned Webster verbal venom from 103,000-plus fans in Michigan Stadium. In that single afternoon, he went from solid defender to breakout star—on his way to becoming arguably the greatest Michigan State Spartan and one of the best defensive players in college football history. Daugherty would eventually call him "the finest football player I've ever seen."

After that game, *Sports Illustrated* honored Webster as its "Lineman of the Week." But many people still aren't sure exactly what position he played. MSU considered him a member of the secondary, and he reported to defensive backs coach Vince Carillot. He lined up most often as a strong-side linebacker and played outside linebacker in the pros. And that's exactly what made Webster the key to MSU's great defenses of 1965 and 1966. At 6'5", 218 pounds and with tremendous speed and strength, he could mix it up on the line (he was a defensive end as a freshman

Duffy Daugherty once said of roverback George Webster: "He doesn't hit people—he explodes them!"

The Untouchable Trio

Most schools and franchises wait several years after a star's playing career is finished to retire the player's number. Michigan State waited about seven months to permanently deny access to George Webster's number 90, in June 1967. That's how much of an impact Webster made in his four years in East Lansing.

The honor is even more impressive considering that number 90 is one of just three MSU football numbers to have been retired. Tackle Don Coleman's number 78 was the first, in 1952. Coleman, a consensus All-American in 1951, was inducted into the College Football Hall of Fame in 1975; Webster joined the hall in 1987.

The third MSU number to be retired is 46, symbolic of John Hannah's forty-six years of service to the school. Hannah, who was MSU's president from 1941 to 1969, was a huge proponent of athletics who turned Michigan State College into Michigan State University and got his school into the Big Ten in 1948. "John Hannah is the greatest legend in the history of Michigan State," former MSU coach George Perles once said.

and sophomore), stuff the run and blitz the quarterback as a line-backer, and drop back and blanket the fastest of receivers.

"He made so many great plays," noted Henry Bullough, Webster's defensive coordinator, "great plays became average."

In MSU's 10–10 tie game with Notre Dame in 1966, Webster spent much of the day covering star receiver Jim Seymour. Seymour finished with zero catches. The season before, when Webster was primarily a run-stopper against the Fighting Irish in South Bend, Notre Dame came up with minus-12 yards rushing and 24 passing for net gain of 12. MSU won 12–3, and Webster gained the bulk of the attention, even on a defense with stars like Bubba Smith, Charlie Thornhill, and Ron Goovert. "He's all over the field, he's able to come from anywhere," lamented Notre Dame offensive tackle Bob Meeker. "Webster hits ball carriers," observed *Chicago Daily News* writer Bill Jauss, "the way the Bears' Dick Butkus does."

Ah yes, the hitting. Reliable tackling statistics do not exist from Webster's era, but stories of his ferocious attacks on ballcarriers are plentiful. Face masks with a vertical bar down the middle for extra protection had become popular for defensive players at the time, but Webster shunned them, going instead with the thin, double-bar around the chin that quarterbacks and receivers favored, in an effort to, he explained, "be a little more imposing" — as if he needed the help.

The knockout shot on Clancy was the first of many memorable collisions for Webster, who also punctured Notre Dame fullback Rocky Bleier's kidney with a hit in 1966. Thornhill's favorite story comes from the 1965 Purdue game, two weeks after Michigan, when Webster knocked a Purdue halfback from the game on the second play. "I thought he killed him," Thornhill remembered with a laugh. Everyone who was around at the time chuckles at the memory of Purdue star quarterback Bob Griese trembling from under center at the sight of Webster approaching. The Spartans roughed him up repeatedly in a 41–20 win in 1966, with Webster delivering a few bone-crunchers. "He doesn't tackle people—he explodes them!" Daugherty once said.

"Unbelievable. Unbelievable. He will hit you so hard—and it's not just one hit, in one game. He will hit you all day long," Thornhill said of Webster. "Jack Tatum could hit too, but they forget George Webster did it all the time. Tatum did it every once in a while."

It had taken Webster a while to get his chance. A lifelong Clemson fan, Webster grew up in Anderson, South Carolina, about 17 miles from Clemson's campus. A prolific athlete at Anderson's Westside High, he led the way for a pair of state football titles, a state basketball title, and earned an individual state championship in the shot put. Clemson coach Frank Howard knew Webster was destined for big things, but southern schools were not yet integrated. So Howard placed a call to Daugherty, one of his close friends in the coaching profession, and Daugherty got involved.

Webster was interested in Minnesota, another school with a reputation for welcoming black athletes, but once he met Daugherty he forgot about the Golden Gophers. "Duffy was a great man, and I loved him," Webster once said of Daugherty, who seemed to have an endless supply of contacts around the nation, plus the personal charm to win more tough recruiting battles than he lost. Daugherty's 1963 class, which might have

Biggie Munn (left) and Duffy Daugherty (right) help George Webster retire his number in 1967.

been his best, included Clinton Jones, Gene Washington, Bubba Smith, Dick Kenney, Pat Gallinagh, Phil Hoag, Jim Summers, Charlie Thornhill, and Jerry West. Webster was less heralded than several of his fellow recruits.

Freshmen were ineligible in those days, so Webster had a year to learn defensive end. Daugherty figured Webster's combination of height, speed, and strength would make him an ideal pass rusher. As a sophomore in 1964 on MSU's disappointing 4–5 team, Webster did well enough to earn himself honorable mention All–Big Ten. But Daugherty decided to mix things up for 1965, and he finally moved Webster to roverback to replace departing senior Charles Migyanka. Daugherty had invented the position in 1958 to give his defense more versatility, and All-America George Saimes played it best in the early 1960s. It was more like a strong safety than anything (MSU played with two cornerbacks and one safety at the time), but Daugherty saw the potential for an expanded role with an athlete like Webster manning it.

"He said, 'You are my monster man.' I wasn't sure what that meant, but I liked the idea right away," Webster recalled years later to the *Detroit News*. "He just wanted me to line up where I thought it was best to be — play the whole field, I guess you'd say. It was a great position, because it allowed me to make a lot of plays. As far as I know, I was the first monster man in football."

Or at least, the most monstrous. Webster had a quiet, polite personality off the field, and he wasn't as much of a talker on it as Smith and Thornhill. "I didn't say much to anyone," Webster said years after his MSU career ended. "I think Duffy must have thought I didn't like him." Daugherty certainly loved what he saw on the field. Webster's incredible day at Michigan, including those five straight unassisted plays and the knockout shot on Clancy, made him MSU's biggest star — and most feared player — in 1965. Fans, writers, and opponents marveled at how he could throw an offensive tackle aside like a rag doll and punish a ballcarrier on one play; blitz and chase down a rolling quarterback from behind on the next; then wrap up the series by lining up outside and breaking up a pass intended for his opponent's fastest receiver. That unpredictability gave opposing coaches migraines during game-planning sessions.

As a junior, Webster certainly benefited from a defense that was stocked with great seniors—Harold Lucas, Bob Viney, Don Bierowicz, and Buddy Owens on the line, Goovert at linebacker, and Don Japinga at cornerback—along with fellow underclassmen Smith, Thornhill, and safety Jess Phillips. Michigan and Notre Dame weren't the only big-name victims of MSU's 1965 front seven—they also held Ohio State to negative rushing yards (minus-22). MSU was named national champion by UPI before losing 14–12 to UCLA in a Rose Bowl, thanks to a pair of UCLA touchdowns that came on short fields after MSU mistakes. That dropped the Spartans to number two in the final AP poll, which that season, for the first time, waited for bowl results.

In 1966 Webster was named defensive captain, replacing Japinga who graduated the year before, and it was up to him to maintain the defense's reputation as one of the nation's best. He did, helping the Spartans finish number two in the nation in total defense for the second season in a row. "He's probably the best player—and hardest hitter—I've ever played with or against," stated Japinga. "And he was a great leader. He didn't say a lot, but when he did, by gosh, everyone listened to him."

In 1965 MSU yielded just 45.6 rushing yards per game and 6.2 points per game, both tops in the nation and the best in school history. In 1966 those numbers rose only slightly, to 51.4 rushing yards and 9.9 points a game, despite heavy personnel losses. Webster's increased leadership role and command of the defensive calls were a key, as was his chemistry with Thornhill. "George would say, 'Which way is [the play] going, Dog?' And I'd say, 'To the right,'" Thornhill recalled. "Between the two of us, we'd have a play read, and then we'd just see who could get there for the tackle first." In the 1966 opener against N.C. State, they got to a ballcarrier behind the line at the same time and started arguing over who was first, until the halfback finally had to yell at them to cut it out so he could get up and go back to the huddle.

Perhaps the most astounding thing about Webster's junior and senior seasons was the fact that he was in near-constant pain. He had to sit out spring ball as a sophomore with a left knee injury, and by his senior season both knees had been battered. Webster had a variety of additional injuries as a Spartan, suffering hamstring pulls and a rather serious rib injury. The trainer's room was his haven before and after games—but never during. MSU knew he would suit up regardless of his physical condition.

"He's one of the most outstanding, gifted, formidable athletes who ever played the game," said Clinton Jones, MSU's star half-back and co-captain in 1966. "He could rise to any occasion, no matter how much pain he was in. If he was hurt, he seemed to play better. If he was healthy, we'd be concerned."

Webster's career ended with the bittersweet 10–10 tie against Notre Dame in the "Game of the Century," wrapping up two seasons that saw MSU go 19–1–1. The Spartans finished number two to the Fighting Irish in both polls. Webster was a unanimous first-team All-American as a junior and senior, and MSU retired his jersey number 90 just months after he left. The Houston Oilers drafted Webster in the first round, number five overall, in the first NFL draft to include the AFL as part of its merger agreement. In a postseason college all-star game, the media quickly singled out Webster as the best pro prospect of the bunch. His

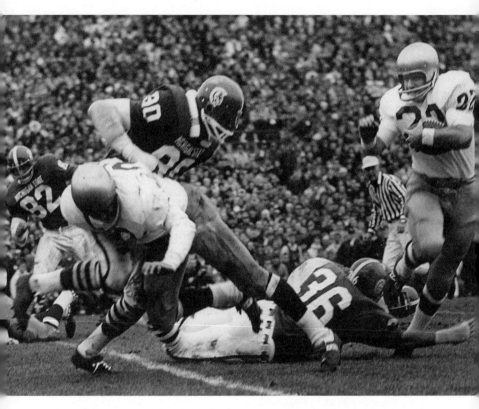

George Webster (90) pushes aside a blocker in the famous 1966 Notre Dame game.

coach on the East team, Tom Cahill, asked Webster before the game which position he'd like to play. "He replied, 'Anywhere,' and he meant it," Cahill said. "He'll be the next Dick Butkus. . . . [o]r I'll be fooled."

Webster made an immediate impact as a hard-hitting outside linebacker with the Oilers, prompting coach Wally Lemm to call him "a once-in-a-lifetime rookie." "I have never seen a line-

Pro-lific

MSU fans have twice voted George Webster Michigan State's best player ever. But Webster wasn't the first player drafted by the NFL out of his MSU senior class. He wasn't the second, either.

In a feat unmatched by another school before or since, MSU had four players taken among the top eight picks of the 1967 NFL draft. Defensive end Bubba Smith went number one overall to Baltimore. Halfback Clinton Jones went number two to Minnesota. Webster went number five to Houston. And receiver Gene Washington went number eight, also to Minnesota. "You might say we had some talent back then," Smith said.

Four other Spartans went in the draft that year: lineman Jeff Richardson (round six, number 146) to the New York Jets; cornerback Jim Summers (round nine, number 217) to Denver; linebacker Charlie Thornhill (round nine, number 232) to the Boston Patriots; and kicker Dick Kenney (round fourteen, number 358) to Philadelphia.

Webster was the AFL Rookie of the Year for Houston, and he played well enough to prompt coach Wally Lemm to say Webster "does some things as well as anyone I've ever seen in pro ball." Webster had a few more great seasons for the Oilers before getting traded to the Steelers, then to the Patriots—a year before the Steelers won their first Super Bowl. He wrapped up an injury-plagued, ten-year pro career in 1976.

"He would have had a lot more success if his knees were better," former MSU defensive coordinator Hank Bullough said of Webster. "He could have been one of the all-time greats."

backer, which is a difficult position to play and takes a couple years to learn, adapt like Webster has," Lemm said. Webster was named AFL Rookie of the Year in 1967, and he had a few more strong years before being shipped to Pittsburgh, then New England. His bad knees ultimately cost him what might have been a legendary pro career. But Webster still made All-AFL three times, was one of four players from the AFL to be All-Pro in 1968, and has a spot in the Pro Football Hall of Fame's All-Time AFL Defensive Team.

After retiring from football in 1976, Webster went into business in Houston, but his health problems continued. Circulation problems in his legs, dating back to his football career, forced doctors to treat him for a blood disorder. He was diagnosed with throat cancer in 1990 and recovered, but he then got prostate cancer. He had triple bypass surgery in 1992 and ultimately had to have both legs amputated because of his circulation problem. Bullough organized a fund-raiser for Webster in 1997, to help him pay for massive medical bills. Webster was deeply touched by the outpouring of support from fans—the same fans who have twice voted him MSU's best football player ever. "When you consider all the great players who have played at Michigan State," Webster said of being named the number one Spartan, "I was just amazed."

The same can be said for anyone who saw George Webster play.

A Tie for the Ages

As the pile of muddy, bloody players broke up and the men slowly rose to return to their sides of the field, George Webster snarled to anyone who would listen: "Are you sissies playing for a tie?" The final seconds of the biggest game college football had ever seen were melting away, and it was painfully clear to all involved that the numbers on the scoreboard—Notre Dame 10, Michigan State 10—were not going to change. Number one Notre Dame and number two MSU were about to finish sixty minutes of brutally violent, beautifully dramatic football. And nothing would be settled. No one would be satisfied.

Notre Dame coach Ara Parseghian had decided to play it safe and keep it on the ground for the final two minutes, rather than risk disaster. He knew his team had another game, against Southern Cal, and that MSU's season was finished—giving Notre Dame an excellent shot at finishing tops in the polls. But that didn't wash with Parseghian's players, not then, not after weeks of national buildup and three hours of laboring for a victory. As Webster and MSU teammates Bubba Smith and Charlie "Mad Dog" Thornhill berated the Notre Dame players for going into a shell, the Irish screamed back, some weeping, swearing that this wasn't their idea. "The coach sent in instructions," Notre Dame quarterback Coley O'Brien said through tears after the game. "He's the boss."

When it was over, most of the 80,011 who packed Spartan Stadium stood in silence for forty-five minutes, as if waiting for some kind of encore. On the field, Smith pleaded with officials to institute an overtime rule, right then and there. Players wandered around dazed, and Parseghian and MSU coach Duffy Daugherty greeted each other briefly, with matching looks of exhaustion and exasperation.

November 19, 1966, was supposed to be it—the day two teams dubbed by many as the best in college football history would determine which was better. It was the first, and still the most appropriate, use of the phrase "Game of the Century." Witnessing the action were 754 journalists, the most ever to cover a sporting event and hundreds more than would show up for the first NFL–AFL Super Bowl in a couple months. The matchup inspired astounding hyperbole from some of the nation's finest publications, as in *Washington Post* reporter William Gildea's pregame story: "If ever there were to be another event to leave the nation as transfixed as on Pearl Harbor Day, 1:30 P.M. Saturday should qualify as a likely time. This is when the football game that will make America stand still begins."

The *Wall Street Journal* weighed in too, with a story on ticket demand. It was estimated that 250,000 tickets could have been sold for the game. They were so hot, a Saginaw man offered up his liquor store for a pair. More than two thousand MSU students applied to join the band that week. And anyone who couldn't make it to East Lansing for the game was bound to watch it on TV. The game had 33 million viewers, a record for college football. It was the first sporting event broadcast live to Hawaii and to troops overseas. An NCAA rule limiting national TV appearances kept the game from going national, because Notre Dame had already been on coast-to-coast in its season opener against Purdue. So ABC received 50,000 letters and a petition signed by 20,000 people, enough to convince the network to show the game on tape delay in the parts of the South and Northwest that wouldn't get it live.

Number one and number two had never met this late in the season. The game featured twenty-five players who would be named All-Americans at some point in their careers, including eighteen first-teamers—twelve for Notre Dame, six for MSU—that season. There were thirty-three future pros on that field, including ten first-round draft picks. Smith, Webster, Thornhill, Clinton Jones, Gene Washington, Jimmy Raye, Jerry West, Jess Phillips, Bob Apisa, Pat Gallinagh, George Chatlos, Nick Jordan,

Best of the Best

It seemed most of America's top college football players were on the field together when MSU and Notre Dame met in 1966. Here is the list of first-team All-Americans from each team that season (both teams also had players that year who earned All-America status in subsequent seasons):

MSU: Bob Apisa, FB; Clinton Jones, HB; Bubba Smith, DE; Gene Washington, E; George Webster, DB; Jerry West, OT.

Notre Dame: Nick Eddy, HB; Jim Lynch, LB; Tom Regner, OG; Alan Page, DE; Pete Duranko, DT; Kevin Hardy, DT; Jim Seymour, E; Paul Seiler, OT; George Goeddeke, C; Tom Schoen, DB; Larry Conjar, FB; Terry Hanratty, QB.

Tony Conti, Phil Hoag, Alan Brenner, and Jeff Richardson starred for the Spartans. Jim Lynch, Rocky Bleier, Alan Page, Pete Duranko, Jim Seymour, Terry Hanratty, Nick Eddy, Larry Conjar, George Goeddeke, Tom Regner, Kevin Hardy, and Coley O'Brien countered for the Irish.

College football had never seen anything like this—the hype, the talent, the intensity, the quality of play on both sides. And now it was all ending in a dreaded tie. The mythical national championship would be left up to the pollsters, and the game itself would be dissected and argued about for decades to come.

The Notre Dame side still bemoans the injuries to key players Hanratty and Eddy. MSU still talks about a pair of questionable calls that might have cost the Spartans the game. And there's no end in sight to their debate.

Thank goodness.

"I guess it was meant to be," Thornhill said nearly forty years later. "It's made this game even bigger. If we would have won the game, it wouldn't be talked about the way it is today. It was the biggest college football game ever. And it changed college football forever."

Soon enough, TV executives were figuring out ways to exert more influence on the game, reaping giant financial benefits from college football in the seventies and beyond. Schools in the South, having seen MSU dominate college football with twelve blacks among its twenty-two starters, would finally start inviting the African Americans in their backyards to stay home and play. But no one involved in the event was thinking about any of that stuff on the chilly, gray November morning. They just wanted to win a football game.

No extra motivation was necessary, but Notre Dame had some. The year before, the Spartans had stormed into South Bend and smothered Parseghian's team 12–3, clinching the national championship in the process. MSU's defense held Notre Dame to negative yardage for the first time in Irish history, and the Spartans let them know all about it. Thornhill, enraged before the game by reports that Notre Dame students were attacking members of MSU's band, tore off his team's locker room door, then banged on Notre Dame's door and implored the Irish to come out for some punishment. After running a hopeless

Irish sweep out of bounds, he even had a few choice words for Parseghian. No one in South Bend had forgotten.

MSU was worked up into a rage as well, thanks mostly to the aforementioned voters. The Spartans started the season ranked number one in both the AP and UPI polls, and they were still there after whipping Michigan 20–7 on October 8. But MSU had to come back for a win the next week on the road, in bad weather, against a tough Ohio State team. The Spartans' 11–8 victory came on the same day number two Notre Dame crushed North Carolina 32–0. The following Monday, the Fighting Irish were sitting at number one, and the newly number two Spartans were grousing about what they perceived as a blatant media bias for Notre Dame. "I've always thought the object of the game was to win," Daugherty said after he saw the polls.

MSU responded by destroying Bob Griese and number nine Purdue 41–20 the following week. On the same day, Notre Dame took apart number ten Oklahoma 38–0. MSU outscored its next three opponents by a combined score of 115–26. Notre Dame ran up a 135–7 tally on its next three. These Irish were a far more dangerous team than the 1965 version, thanks to the sophomore pass-catch combo of quarterback Terry Hanratty and end Jim Seymour. Freshmen were still ineligible to play, or both players likely would have seen the field straight out of high school. The two arrived with such a bang in 1966, they made the cover of *Time* magazine by midseason.

The Spartans had heard quite enough about Hanratty-to-Seymour by game week. The Irish, meanwhile, were focused on MSU star halfback Clinton Jones, a two-time first team All-American who rushed for 784 yards that season.

It's a wonder either team was able to prepare properly, considering the crush of national attention both endured that week. Writers and broadcasters, among them a young ABC reporter named Peter Jennings, swarmed both campuses. A writer named Brent Musburger represented the *Chicago American*. Big names like Jimmy Breslin, Paul Zimmerman, and Bill Gleason were keenly interested in the outcome of the game. At Notre Dame's weekly news conference, a reporter from MSU's student publication, *The State News*, asked Parseghian how he planned to deal with MSU's "formidable defense." Parseghian promptly banned the reporter from speaking with his players.

On the MSU campus, many professors threw up their arms by midweek and canceled classes. Students held impromptu rallies outside the dorm-room windows of their gridiron heroes. In one such episode, Bubba Smith finally opened his window and looked out on a large contingent of his classmates. They began to chant "Speech! Speech! Speech!" Bubba tried to think of something to say, and he famously began with, "Uhhhhhh . . ." That was enough. The students broke into a roar, as if Bubba had just announced plans to run for office.

By Friday, the anticipation was feverish. And it was a harrowing day for both teams. Notre Dame's All-America halfback, Nick Eddy, was already playing with a tender shoulder. He stumbled as he got off the train in East Lansing, aggravating the injury, and Eddy was scratched from the game. MSU almost suffered a huge loss of its own when Bubba Smith was arrested on Friday night for unpaid parking tickets. An East Lansing officer pulled Smith over and decided to haul him in. A few hours later, Bubba was bailed out by MSU athletic director Biggie Munn,

Different Shades of Green

The "Game of the Century" on November 19, 1966, is the most famous link between MSU and Notre Dame, but these old rivals have a long, often surprising history.

Legendary Notre Dame coach Knute Rockne nearly took the Michigan State (then called MAC) job in 1918, before the Notre Dame job opened up. But in 1921 Rockne actually signed a contract with MAC, according to the *Detroit Times*. He was set to leave Notre Dame for a three-year deal starting at $4,500 a year, but the Irish countered, and Rockne decided to stay in South Bend.

MAC center Lyman Frimodig (1915–16) was a boyhood friend of Irish legend George Gipp in Calumet, Michigan, and he nearly convinced Gipp to join him in East Lansing.

Jim Crowley, one of Notre Dame's famed Four Horsemen, coached Michigan State from 1929 to 1932, compiling a 22–8–3 record. His line coach was Frank Leahy, who would later become one of Notre Dame's most successful head coaches. Crowley and Leahy left Michigan State in 1933 for Fordham, where they coached Vince Lombardi and the "Seven Blocks of Granite."

Former Notre Dame coach Tyrone Willingham played quarterback for MSU, and former Notre Dame coach Dan Devine was an MSU assistant coach for Biggie Munn and Duffy Daugherty.

Daugherty turned down the Notre Dame head coaching job in 1963.

who had some choice words for the police on his way out.

Bad karma, it seemed, had found both teams. The game couldn't come soon enough. The waiting had become almost unbearable for the coaches, players, fans, and media who had built the event into something much larger than sixty minutes of football: "Intercollegiate football reaches its finest hour here tomorrow," wrote George Strickler of the *Chicago Tribune*. "Never before in ninety-seven years of collegiate competition has a season built up to a climax that had such universal appeal."

One of Daugherty's traditions for home game days was to attend 6:30 A.M. Mass with his Catholic players. This Saturday was no different—except for the relatively small amount of sleep everyone had gotten—and Daugherty and players like Bob Apisa, Pat Gallinagh, Dick Kenney, and Clinton Jones attended as usual. Typically the streets at this time of day would be barren and quiet, but not on this day. "It was incredible," Apisa remembered. "There were banners all over the place and hordes of people walking through the streets and on campus. At 6:30 in the morning! You could just feel the intensity."

Emotion was boiling over by the time Daugherty and his players returned to their on-campus hotel, the Kellogg Center, for the pregame breakfast. When the Spartans left the hotel for their ritual walk along the Red Cedar River to Spartan Stadium, some of them were moved to tears. In the locker room, Gallinagh was moved to permanently disable a locker with his head. Thornhill crafted an "ND" symbol out of some white tape and stuck it on the front of his helmet—right where he planned to meet the Irish.

It was time. Time to find out if MSU's fearsome defense could stop the Hanratty-to-Seymour aerial show. Time to find out if Notre Dame could clamp down on Clinton Jones and MSU's versatile quarterback, Jimmy Raye. Time to find out which team would be labeled as college football's greatest ever: the defending national champion Spartans or the five-point-favorites Fighting Irish?

Notre Dame won the toss and elected to receive. MSU's defense held, amid chants of "Kill, Bubba, kill!" from delirious Spartan fans. Notre Dame then stuffed the Spartans on their first offensive series, and it was clear that points would come sparingly. When Notre Dame got the ball back, Hanratty found Bob Gladieux downfield on a third-and-10, placing the ball at MSU's 36. As it turned out, that would be Hanratty's only completion of the day.

On second-and-9, Hanratty took off on a quarterback draw. Thornhill met him first at the 35, wrapped him, and turned him—right into a 6'7", 290-pound truck named Bubba Smith. Smith smeared Hanratty into the ground, crushing his left shoulder in the process. Hanratty tried to tough it out, staying in the game and throwing an incompletion on the next play, but after that he knew he was done. Enter little-known sophomore backup Coley O'Brien. "The thing is, we had prepared ourselves for Hanratty, we knew he stared down his primary receiver, and we felt good about stopping him," Thornhill noted. "And we knew nothing about Coley O'Brien, who was a much better runner."

Notre Dame's center, George Goeddeke, went down with a knee injury two plays later, and the Irish were suddenly limping through the game, halfway through the first quarter. MSU capitalized on its third possession, late in the opening period. Raye found Washington for 42 yards, down to the Notre Dame 31.

Notre Dame quarterback Terry Hanratty (5) was gone in the first quarter with a separated shoulder—courtesy of Bubba Smith.

Three plays later, on fourth-and-inches, Raye sneaked ahead for 2 yards to the Notre Dame 20. The first quarter ended with MSU mounting the first real threat.

Much had been made of Nick Eddy's injury and its effect on Notre Dame's offense, but the absence of MSU fullback Bob Apisa was an overlooked factor in the game. Apisa's knee had been injured three weeks earlier against Northwestern, and he was sitting on the sideline now as MSU's offense drove. Apisa was fast and powerful, a first team All-American that season, and he actually led MSU with 5.2 yards a carry and nine rushing touchdowns. Apisa would eventually try to give it a go early in the third quarter, but he quickly realized he wasn't able.

Not for the Timid

MSU and Notre Dame both entered the 1966 game with key injuries: All-America halfback Nick Eddy for Notre Dame and All-America fullback Bop Apisa for MSU. Several teammates joined them on the sidelines before the violent contest was over.

Notre Dame quarterback Terry Hanratty separated his shoulder and had to leave the game early in the first quarter. MSU linebacker Charlie "Mad Dog" Thornhill hit him first, and defensive end Bubba Smith smashed him into the turf, causing the injury.

Two plays later, MSU safety Jess Phillips hit Notre Dame center George Goeddeke in the knee on a botched Notre Dame punt. Goeddeke was done for the day.

MSU fullback Reggie Cavender, Apisa's backup, suffered a shoulder injury in the first quarter but still managed to score his team's only touchdown two plays later.

Midway through the third quarter, Phillips struck again with the hit of the day. On a crossing route, Phillips hurled himself into Notre Dame receiver Bob Gladieux, leaving Gladieux writhing in pain on the field. The hit was so forceful, it shattered Gladieux's quadricep.

A shoulder injury claimed MSU starting guard Mitchell Pruiett in the fourth quarter.

Notre Dame fullback Rocky Bleier played the whole game but discovered later that he had a lacerated kidney, the result of a crushing hit from MSU roverback George Webster.

In Apisa's place was sophomore Reggie Cavender. MSU realized by now that Notre Dame was shading Jones's every move, so Cavender got the call on the first play of the second quarter. He rumbled for 11 yards to the Notre Dame 9. On the next play, first-and-goal, Cavender got 5 more, hurting his shoulder in the process. The Spartans tried Jones on second down, but the Irish ganged up and dropped him for no gain. So on third-and-goal from the 4, Raye handed to Cavender, who went right and followed a crushing block by Jones. Cavender barreled into the end zone, and after Dick Kenney's extra point, the Spartans led 7–0 with 13:20 to play in the first half. It was the first touchdown allowed by Notre Dame's defense since the first game of the season against Purdue.

MSU's defense then forced another three-and-out, and when Raye took off on a 30-yard scamper, the crowd sensed a route. On second-and-9 from the Notre Dame 36, Raye dropped back to pass and threw errantly into the hands of Notre Dame linebacker Jim Lynch. That's when Jones made one of the game's most important *defensive* plays. He dove at Lynch, driving his shoulder pads into Lynch's midsection and knocking the ball out. Jones then recovered the fumble, and MSU had itself a rather unconventional first down. The Irish held, though, and four plays later Dick Kenney nailed a 47-yard field goal for a 10–0 advantage.

At this point it looked like Notre Dame's offense wouldn't have a chance. MSU defensive coordinator Hank Bullough was lining up Bubba Smith at nose guard, in part so he could get defensive end George Chatlos on the field more, and in part to disrupt Notre Dame's interior blocking schemes. But Coley O'Brien had settled down by now, and his ability to move outside

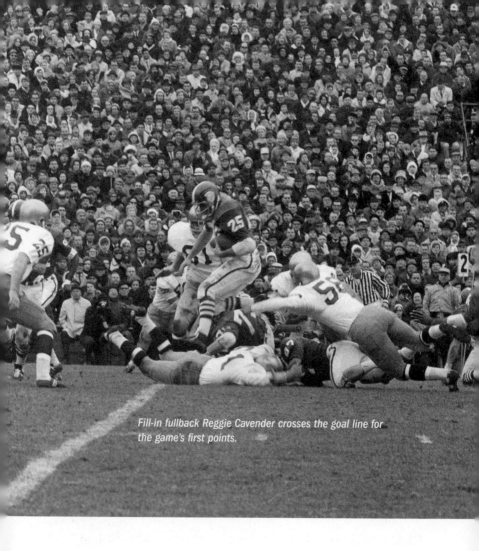

Fill-in fullback Reggie Cavender crosses the goal line for the game's first points.

of the pocket started to bother MSU's defense. He hit Bob Gladieux for 9 yards. Then he found sophomore star Seymour alone downfield, but Seymour—who would not catch a pass all day—dropped the ball. O'Brien kept coming, though, hitting Rocky Bleier for 11.

Then, on second-and-10 from the MSU 34, O'Brien dropped back, slid to his right, and saw Gladieux streaking toward the end zone on a post pattern. O'Brien let it fly, and MSU safety Jess Phillips, who had been coaxed out of position by Seymour, raced toward Gladieux. Phillips dove and missed the ball by inches. It fell into Gladieux's hands for a touchdown, stunning everyone in Spartan Stadium and cutting MSU's lead to 10–7 with 4:30 left in the second quarter.

Although the scoring was all but finished for the day, the second half was full of action, drama, and, of course, controversy. On MSU's first play from scrimmage in the third quarter, Clint Jones lost a fumble that Notre Dame recovered at MSU's 31. Parseghian called for a throw to the end zone on first down, but O'Brien left it short, and Phillips intercepted.

That's how it would go for the rest of the afternoon—MSU's offense leaving MSU's defense in precarious positions, and MSU's defense saving the day. Webster came up huge midway through the third when he met Notre Dame fullback Larry Conjar at the line, knocking Conjar backward and forcing the ball to pop out and go flying. Cornerback Sterling Armstrong covered the ball, and the Spartans and their fans celebrated wildly—until they noticed the red flag (they were red then, not yellow) lying on the field. The call was offsides on Bubba Smith, and the play was negated, although replays appear to show that Smith merely got a great jump and left before his linemates—but not before the snap. MSU even had a film session for reporters a few days later to prove as much, but it didn't matter on Saturday.

Notre Dame had new life, and with the third quarter winding down the Irish moved inside MSU's 20. On third-and-3 from the 10, O'Brien dropped back to pass. MSU's pass rush flushed him out of the pocket, and he rolled right and found a huge opening. O'Brien had a path to the end zone, but MSU tackle Jeff Richardson closed it off, lunging and grabbing O'Brien by the arm, then yanking him to the ground for no gain. The third quarter ended on what might have been the game-saving play.

Kicker Joe Azzaro opened the fourth quarter by knocking through a 27-yard field goal, and the Irish celebrated their hard-earned comeback. Momentum was on Notre Dame's side now, and its defense appeared impregnable. Raye threw an interception to Notre Dame safety Tom Schoen at midfield. The MSU defense held. Raye threw another interception to Schoen, again at midfield, on a deep pass intended for Alan Brenner. This time Schoen weaved his way for a big return to MSU's 18. With about six minutes to play in the game, the Fighting Irish were in position to win.

But MSU's defense would come up with yet another answer. On second-and-8 from the 16, MSU end Phil Hoag broke through the line and dropped Notre Dame backup halfback Dave Haley for a loss of 8. On the next play, Bubba Smith got through and tipped O'Brien's pass, which was headed for a wide-open Bleier. Notre Dame was left with a 41-yard field goal attempt by Azzaro that sailed wide right.

The MSU offense couldn't move, though, and it had to punt with less than two minutes to play, setting up questionable call number two. Dick Kenney's punt sailed toward Schoen, who called for a fair catch at his 30. Schoen dropped the ball, and it appeared MSU recovered. But the officials didn't bother to see who had jumped on the ball; they ruled Schoen had caught it first, ending the play, and then dropped it. Review of the film later appeared to show that Schoen never had control.

With disaster averted, the Fighting Irish sat about 40 yards away from a reasonable attempt at a winning field goal, with 1:24 left on the clock. And Parseghian decided to run the ball. His team was regaled with boos and vicious insults from the Spartans. "We might have lost the game with a pass at that point," Parseghian explained after the game. "If we had lost the ball, say on an interception, it might have cost us the game. And I wasn't about to do a jackass thing like that."

Parseghian was concerned about Kenney's range. He also knew his team would have a chance to solidify its number one ranking the next week against Southern Cal, while MSU sat at home. But the idea that he packed it in completely is a misconception. The Irish moved 9 yards in their first three plays, then faced a fourth-and-1 at their own 39, with about 30 seconds left. Parseghian went for it, fearing disaster if he tried to punt. O'Brien got 2 yards on a sneak. MSU then frantically called its second timeout. On first down, Parseghian called for a pass, figuring his team was in good enough field position to give it a shot. But Bubba Smith crashed through the line and dropped O'Brien for a loss of 7, then called MSU's final timeout.

Five seconds remained, and Parseghian wasn't about to do anything crazy. O'Brien ran for 5 yards, the clock hit zero, the fans booed lustily, Smith begged for overtime, Parseghian and Daugherty trudged to midfield for a limp handshake, and players on both sides stumbled into their respective locker rooms, unsatisfied. The anti-Parseghian backlash was intense, and it remained so for years afterward.

No one liked the look of this scoreboard at the time, but the result ensured the contest's immortality.

"They'll get a national championship for quitting," Clinton Jones told reporters in the locker room.

"Outlined against a blue-gray October sky, the four mice went into hiding again today," wrote Jim Murray of the *Los Angeles Times,* playing off Grantland Rice's famous ode to the Four Horsemen.

"NOTRE DAME RUNS OUT THE CLOCK AGAINST MICHIGAN STATE," proclaimed the cover of *Sports Illustrated.*

Parseghian kept taking abuse, but his strategy paid off. The polls were split the Monday after the game, but Notre Dame finished number one in both after thrashing number ten USC 51–0 to end the season.

Four independent selectors, including the National Football Foundation, picked MSU as national champs, but that was little consolation. "It's a feeling you can never describe," remembered Thornhill, who led all players with 16 tackles in the game. "It took weeks to get over that."

A forty-year reunion of the players was scheduled for September 23, 2006, at Spartan Stadium, during another MSU–Notre Dame game. Nearly a half-century after the "Game of the Century," the Spartans and Fighting Irish would finally be able to meet as teams and talk—maybe even argue—about the extraordinary events of November 19, 1966.

"It will be exciting to meet those guys personally for the first time," Apisa said. "We didn't really mingle much after the game, like you would normally do. Everyone was just kind of wandering around the field in shock."

Gibby

Before recruiting "experts" gave themselves jobs and built Web sites to assign rankings to seventeen-year-olds who are analyzed down to their choice of lunch pail, college football coaches had film. Glorious, grainy film. They heard about prospects from friends in the coaching business. A tip here, a tip there, trips to outlying areas to find hidden, rurally raised gems. No videotapes, no DVDs, no Internet reports detailing a prospect's list of offers and latest whim. Just reels of footage and major cracks for worthy players to slip through.

That's how a guy like Kirk Gibson nearly played in the Mid-American Conference.

Andy MacDonald is not a name that resonates with most Michigan State fans. But it was MacDonald's keen eye, in the midst of a late-night session with a projector in his office, that made the way for Gibson to become one of Michigan State's most celebrated sports figures. An assistant to head coach Denny Stolz, MacDonald was scouting a target from West Bloomfield High in the fall of 1974 when he noticed a tailback from one of West Bloomfield's opponents, Waterford Kettering. He looked good, fast, tough. Worth another look, perhaps.

Soon enough, Gibson had an offer from MSU. He had planned on accepting a scholarship from Central Michigan, but he was thrilled to hear from East Lansing, where his mother grew up and his grandmother still lived.

Gibson worked to increase his speed in the summer before his freshman season, and he arrived on campus ready to compete for playing time. He was one of the least heralded members of MSU's 1975 recruiting class. An add-on. A dark horse. A guy who might be a decent special teams player some day.

By the time fall camp was finished, Gibson was a starting receiver. He had outrun and outhit his teammates from day one. In the second game of his career, Gibson caught a 56-yard touchdown pass from quarterback Charlie Baggett to beat Miami (Ohio) 14–13. He had nine catches in Stolz's run-dominated offense that year, four of them for touchdowns.

In the third game of Gibson's sophomore season, now playing in new coach Darryl Rogers's wide-open offense, he caught five passes for 173 yards. People were starting to realize that this

Lightly regarded when he arrived, Kirk Gibson left MSU as one of the school's most dominating athletes of all time.

was an extraordinary talent. In his junior year, Gibson decided to give the baseball team a try, and he ended up leading MSU to the Big Ten title by hitting .390 in forty-six games, with 52 RBIs, 16 homers, including a few legendary moon shots, and 21 stolen bases in 22 attempts. He immediately became a high-level major league prospect, and that spring he was drafted in the first round by the Detroit Tigers.

The following fall, Gibson led the Spartans to the 1978 Big Ten football title, finishing his career with a league-record 2,347 receiving yards. At 6'3", 215 chiseled pounds, and 4.28 speed in the 40, Gibson could have been the number one overall pick in the Major League Baseball or NFL draft, if he was clearly devoted to one sport.

All this from a guy nobody recruited.

"He is as fine an athlete," Rogers said, "as you would ever hope to coach in a lifetime."

And Gibson was a central figure in one of the most memorable years in Michigan State sports history—his out-of-nowhere display on the diamond in the spring; his gridiron dominance in the fall for MSU's first Big Ten championship team in twelve years; and the basketball national championship in March 1979 for Magic Johnson, Greg Kelser, and coach Jud Heathcote. They beat Larry Bird and Indiana State for the title in what is still the highest-rated college basketball game ever.

Gibson, of course, went on to baseball glory and unforgettable World Series home runs with the Tigers and Los Angeles Dodgers. He had a lot of great years as a professional athlete. But that 1978 football season was special for Gibson and MSU fans. It was a season Rogers had been building toward. And it was a sea-

The Other Switch Hitter

The Michigan State baseball program has produced some major league talent over the years, including Robin Roberts, Dick Radatz, Ron Perranoski, and Mark Mulder. But its most famous baseball alums are a pair of guys who also played some football.

Kirk Gibson, of course, is remembered by MSU fans as the best receiver and one of the best players in the school's gridiron history. He starred for the 1978 Big Ten champions, then went on to major league greatness with the Detroit Tigers and Los Angeles Dodgers.

Spartan fans, however, may not remember Steve Garvey's time in a helmet and shoulder pads in East Lansing. Garvey arrived at MSU from Tampa, Florida, on a baseball scholarship in 1966, and he played for MSU's freshman football team in the fall—making him a part of one of the greatest teams in college football history. The next fall, Garvey moved up to varsity. He was solid as a backup defensive back for Duffy Daugherty, making twenty-two solo tackles and setting himself up for a starting job in 1968 and 1969.

That would not come to pass, however. Garvey exploded as a baseball sophomore under coach Danny Litwhiler in the spring of 1968, hitting .376 and earning a contract from the Los Angeles Dodgers. He went on to star for two decades in the pros, and he and Gibson met in the 1984 World Series. Gibson's Tigers beat Garvey's Padres in five games.

son he began to fear wasn't going to materialize as the summer of 1978 got hot.

A few of MSU baseball coach Danny Litwhiler's players who knew Gibson from high school told Litwhiler he could play. Litwhiler asked Gibson to try out, and Rogers liked the idea—it's not like his senior receiver really needed spring practice. But a couple months in, with the buzz about Gibson's baseball prowess mounting, that decision was looking risky. It was pretty much the opposite of Gibson's high school recruitment. Pro baseball scouts were showing up and calling in droves, watching his every move as the June draft approached.

"If I had to compare him to anybody, he's like Mickey Mantle," Paul Snyder, the Atlanta Braves minor league administrator, said at the time. "You don't see that combination of speed and power very often."

The Braves had the number one overall pick and wanted to use it on Gibson, but the chance that he might opt for the NFL convinced them to take Bob Horner instead (not a bad pick, either). Meanwhile, the Tigers had invited Gibson to Tiger Stadium to take some batting practice. After an hour of watching him launch bombs into the upper deck, Tigers president Jim Campbell was convinced. Detroit drafted Gibson in the first round, despite the football risk, and gave him a $200,000 bonus.

Gibson was elated. Rogers was anxious. With his franchise receiver headed to Lakeland, Florida, for rookie ball, Rogers let a nightmare scenario play through his head: Gibson tears it up in Florida. The Tigers get into a pennant race and tap the rookie for his bat and speed in September. Gibson forgets all about MSU, and the chance for a Big Ten championship is gone with him. "I wish Kirk the best," Rogers said then, "but I sure hope he's playing football for Michigan State next fall. I know he's going to be a pro some day. He's got the whole world in his hands right now."

As it turned out, Gibson hit .250 in Lakeland, the Tigers didn't sniff the pennant, and it wouldn't have mattered anyway.

Gibson tried baseball on a whim in 1978, and within weeks pro scouts were comparing him to Mickey Mantle.

"I'm not going to miss football when I'm finished with this season," Gibson told the *Detroit Free Press* early in his senior campaign. "But there is no way I would have agreed to pass up this season. Baseball and the Tigers would have to wait, or forget about me."

How could Gibson not be excited? This figured to be MSU's best team since Duffy Daugherty roamed the sidelines in the 1960s. Rogers had arrived from San Jose State in 1976, a hotshot coach with a laid-back demeanor and wide-open offense unlike anything seen before in the Big Ten. He replaced Stolz, who was fired in light of NCAA recruiting violations committed by assistant coach Howard Weyers. MSU got three years of probation for the transgressions, which included a ban on bowl games and national TV appearances and a reduction in scholarships. Despite those disadvantages, Rogers had the ingredients for a big third season.

The Rogers Way

Darryl Rogers came to Michigan State to revive a football program crippled by scandal. He bolted four years later for Arizona State, leaving MSU to rebuild again. But in that short tenure, he changed Big Ten football forever.

Darryl Rogers challenged the Big Ten's stodgy-offense tradition and won.

"Darryl Rogers brought passing to the Big Ten," said Jim Hinesly, an All–Big Ten tackle for Rogers's 1978 Big Ten championship team. "People say it was Mike White at Illinois, but in reality it was Darryl Rogers."

Rogers arrived in 1976 to replace Denny Stolz, who was fired after MSU was put on probation for recruiting violations committed by one of Stolz's assistants. Soon enough, the offense Rogers brought with him from San Jose State was being cursed by Big Ten defensive coordinators and copied by offensive coordinators.

The 1978 team set a Big Ten record with 481.3 yards per game and scored 37.4 points per game—still a school record some thirty years later. Rogers's attack featured passing elements not seen before in a league dominated by Woody Hayes, Bo Schembechler, and mind-numbingly boring offensive schemes. Rogers threw to his backs. He sent as many as five pass-catchers out at once. His receivers often used picks from each other to get open. And he let his quarterback read the defense and call plays at the line.

"I'd say most of our plays were called at the line," recalled quarterback Eddie Smith, who had Rogers's full confidence as a senior in 1978. "I'd just say 'Check with me' in the huddle and call out the numbers based on what I saw. We had all played together for so long by then, we were able to communicate like that."

The most important element, of course, was personnel. Smith had three NFL-caliber targets running open on nearly every play: tight end Mark Brammer, receiver Eugene Byrd, and receiver Kirk Gibson. Gibson finished his career with 24 receiving touchdowns, 5 of them for more than 80 yards, 8 for more than 50 yards, and a career average of 21 yards per catch.

After Arizona State, Rogers went on to an unsuccessful stint with the Detroit Lions. The biggest criticism of Rogers? His offense was too conservative.

It started with Gibson, of course, but he wasn't the only offensive difference-maker. Senior quarterback Eddie Smith, a third-year starter, was a precise passer and accomplished reader of defenses. He had freedom unlike most quarterbacks in college football—then or now—at the line of scrimmage. That quarterback control was a key component of Rogers's offense, as was the idea of flooding the field with pass-catchers, including backs, to find gaps in the zone defenses most teams favored. Considering the other receivers—star speedster Eugene Byrd and sure-handed tight end Mark Brammer, both future NFL players—Smith typically had more than one wide-open option.

He also had a strong offensive line, anchored by first team All–Big Ten left tackle Jim Hinesly. The Spartans' kickers, punter Ray Stachowicz and place kicker Morten Andersen, were as fine a tandem as any in the nation. And MSU's defense was solid and underrated, with defensive tackle Mel Land, linebacker Dan Bass, and safety Tommy Graves. "I didn't know we had a defense," Hinesly joked. "I used to tell them, 'All you have to do is break serve once, and we'll win.' "

It looked that way in the 1978 season opener at Purdue when MSU jumped out to a 14–0 lead. But Smith broke his hand scoring the second touchdown, and that's where a potentially historic season was foiled. The Spartans' offense was punchless without Smith, and the Boilermakers came back to win 21–14. MSU recovered by blowing out Syracuse, and Smith returned two weeks later at Southern Cal. But he wasn't ready to throw the ball, and MSU lost 30–9. Smith started getting his feel back the next week, throwing for 307 yards against Notre Dame, but MSU dropped a tight one, 29–25. The Spartans were 1–3, with a trip to play number five and unbeaten Michigan in Ann Arbor up next.

There was no reason for anyone outside of East Lansing to think MSU could avoid its ninth straight loss to the Wolverines. But the Spartans knew better. Smith was finally fully recovered, and Bo Schembechler's Michigan defense was woefully ill prepared to deal with Rogers's offense. The Wolverines were built to stop plodding rushing attacks like their own. Their pass rush was minimal. Their coverage schemes were inadequate. And when Schembechler dropped extra people into coverage, Rogers countered with successful draw plays to tailbacks Steve Smith and Leroy McGee.

The Spartans built a 17–0 halftime lead and held on for a 24–15 victory that was more lopsided than the score suggests. MSU had a 305–132 yardage edge at halftime and finished with perfect balance: 248 yards passing, 248 yards rushing. Gibson had five grabs for 82 yards. Brammer had seven for 79. Byrd had just one catch, but it was a key 20-yarder to keep a drive alive in the second half. "I told coach Rogers before the game he had four of the best guys in the country for what he wanted to do," a contrite Schembechler said afterward. "And those four guys were outstanding today."

And they wouldn't let the Spartans sniff defeat again. Six games remained on the schedule, and all six were absolute thrashings. MSU beat Indiana, Wisconsin, Illinois, Minnesota, Northwestern, and Iowa by an average score of 48–9. That 1–3 start turned into an 8–3 finish, including a 7–1 Big Ten record and share of the school's first league championship since 1966. More than one member of that team thinks 8–3 would have been 11–0 if Eddie Smith had never hurt his hand. The Spartans tied the Wolverines for the championship and held the tiebreaker, but the probation allowed the Wolverines to head to Pasadena.

As difficult as that was for the Spartans to stomach, they had championship rings. And they got them in style, unleashing an offense that was almost laughably dominant once it fully clicked. MSU set a Big Ten record with 481.3 yards of total offense per game and a school record that still stands with 37.4 points per game. Smith threw for then-gaudy numbers of 2,226 yards and 20 touchdowns, 6 to Gibson and 6 to Byrd. Gibson had 42 catches for 806 yards, and he made plays that made people wonder aloud: Is this guy sure he wants to play baseball?

"We saw mostly zone that season, but there were teams that tried to play some man-to-man against us—teams that must have been crazy," Smith remembered. "If I came up to the line and saw man coverage, I couldn't help but look at Gibson and break into a big smile. Nobody could watch Gibson. I mean nobody."

On the first play of the Indiana game, Smith hit Gibson on a crossing pattern and watched the receiver blow past a series of hapless Hoosiers en route to an 86-yard touchdown. It was one of five 80-yard-plus scoring grabs in Gibson's career. "He adds a whole new dimension to the game," Indiana coach Lee Corso said after the game.

"He would make a magnificent pro football player. Right now. For almost any team you name. He's that good," wrote columnist George Puscas of the *Detroit Free Press*, who essentially pleaded publicly for Gibson to pick the NFL after watching him torch the Hoosiers for 146 yards on three catches.

Puscas was not alone. The Spartans were banned from national TV, so Gibson did not get the exposure he deserved. But

Grabs like this had NFL teams courting Gibson, even after his pro baseball career began.

the scouts were showing up to see for themselves. Although Gibson had signed with the Tigers, a number of NFL teams considered taking him in the later rounds, just in case he changed his mind at some point. And if he'd never picked up a bat, Gibson might have been the NFL's number one overall pick. "If there were ratings compiled on 'best athlete' in college football," said Gil Brandt, then a scout for the Dallas Cowboys, "Gibson would probably be number one."

He was the kind of athlete who regularly made his teammates question what they had just seen. MSU liked to run reverses to Gibson, usually on a sweep right that wound up with Gibson going left. Hinesly, the left tackle, was supposed to sell the sweep right, then crack back to take care of anyone who might be in the way. Problem was, Gibson was so fast he was past Hinesly before the tackle could turn to help. "Eventually, I just stopped selling the play right and started running downfield to take people out," Hinesly said. "He'd pass me after about five yards, but at least I had a chance to help him a little bit that way."

One of the most memorable plays Gibson made at MSU was a defensive one. In his next-to-last game at Spartan Stadium, MSU had driven inside the 10 on Minnesota and was poised to score. Eddie Smith pitched right to Steve Smith, who was hit as the ball got to him. A Minnesota defensive back grabbed the ball out of the air and took off for what appeared to be an easy touchdown. Gibson was lined up as a decoy wide left on the play and was in the corner of the end zone, across the field diagonally and at least 15 yards back, when the Minnesota player took off. Yet the Spartan Stadium crowd and both sidelines watched in awe as Gibson turned on the speed, passing every other player on the field in the process, and finally caught and dragged down the Gopher at MSU's 40. For all of MSU's highlights that season, the Gibson tackle was the first one on the reel at the team banquet. "That play," Hinesly said years later, "was incredible."

It was a display of Gibson's physical gifts. It was also a glimpse at his ultra-competitive mindset. Throughout college and his professional career, Gibson was known for his intense—sometimes nasty—personality. He would slam a teammate against a locker. He would seek immediate payback on a safety who had hit him hard on the previous play. He would yell at a coach if necessary. "Gib was Gib," Smith said with a chuckle. "He was always fiery. And he was always open, too. If you didn't believe him, all you had to do was ask him."

In the spring, as Gibson worked to turn himself into a pro baseball player, the St. Louis football Cardinals drafted Gibson in the seventh round. In the summer of 1980 a serious wrist injury ended Gibson's season with the Tigers and appeared to threaten his future in baseball as well. Torn cartilage left some doubt as to whether he would ever be able to swing a bat effectively again. That fall Gibson did color commentary on MSU football games with George Blaha, and football was in his brain again. The Cardinals took a run, and he listened. But the wrist healed perfectly, Gibson went on to October greatness, and football was behind him for good.

The questions are just as enticing today, though. What if Andy MacDonald hadn't spotted Gibson on the flickering screen? What if Eddie Smith hadn't broken his hand against Purdue? And what if Kirk Gibson hadn't shrugged his shoulders and played a season of baseball for the Spartans?

"There's no doubt about it, he would have been just as dominant in pro football," Smith said. "The only difference is, his career wouldn't have been as long."

Gang Green Grips the Big Ten

Another disappointing season was staring Michigan State in the face. But for the moment, the only thing the Spartans could see was coach George Perles—his face reddening to approximate the pink walls of the visiting locker room in Iowa's Kinnick Stadium, his words surpassing, in venom and volume, anything these players had heard from him before.

MSU, 1–2 after blowout losses to Notre Dame and Florida State, trailed rebuilding Iowa 14–7 at the half on October 3, 1987. The Hawkeyes had gone ahead late in the second quarter after recovering a fumble by MSU star tailback Lorenzo White. And Perles, who generally dismissed profane pep talks as contrived, was giving one because he simply couldn't help himself. "I just went overboard. Normally at halftime we make corrections and adjustments, but in that particular game I blew up," Perles said years later. "If you do it very often it might not work, but this time it got their attention."

Perles had to do something. He had asked MSU fans to judge him after five seasons; this was his fifth team. This was the job he had always coveted, the program he always imagined he could return to glory. A native of Detroit's tough Vernor Highway area, Perles had played tackle for MSU for part of one season, 1958, under coach Duffy Daugherty. A knee injury suffered against Wisconsin ended Perles's playing career prematurely, but with Daugherty's help he got into coaching. He was on Daugherty's MSU staff for five seasons and then moved on to the NFL in 1972 as Chuck Noll's defensive line coach with the Steelers. It was there Perles made a name for himself.

Before the 1974 AFC title game against Oakland, Perles added a wrinkle to the Pittsburgh defense, slanting tackles Ernie Holmes and "Mean" Joe Greene in on the center—taking out the center and both guards and allowing middle linebacker Jack Lambert to roam freely and make plays. Oakland never figured it out and rushed for 27 yards; the Steelers dominated and went on to the first of four Super Bowl wins; and Perles later named his defense the "Stunt 4-3." He brought it with him to MSU in 1983, when he replaced Muddy Waters as coach. (Waters, a surprise hire in 1980 when many expected Perles to get the nod, had gone 10–23 in three seasons.)

Perles rebuilt the MSU program steadily, going 23–22–1 in his first four seasons, but impatience was starting to creep into the atmosphere around Spartan Stadium. The 1987 Spartans had high expectations, thanks to a talented defense and an offense led by Lorenzo White, a legitimate Heisman Trophy candidate, and receiver Andre Rison. And MSU was determined to erase the memories of 1986, when four losses by 3 points apiece crushed their hopes of a Big Ten title. The key moment then was a 24–21 loss to number eleven Iowa, when senior quarterback Dave Yarema threw an interception on first down from the Iowa 3, with 1:32 left in the game. Later, head-scratching losses to Indiana and Northwestern left the Spartans with a 6–5 record and no bowl game.

The 1986 Iowa defeat was also marked by a knee injury for White, who had set the single-season MSU rushing record as a sophomore in 1985 with 2,066 yards. White missed the next two games and had just 54 carries the rest of the 1986 season. But he was back healthy for the 1987 season and a run at some lofty senior goals. "The Rose Bowl for us and the Heisman for me," he said before the season.

It started auspiciously enough. The opener was also the first night game in Spartan Stadium history, a nationally televised Monday night game on Labor Day. It was called "The Great American Football Celebration" and came complete with fireworks and Lee Greenwood singing "God Bless the USA." Number sixteen Southern Cal against number twenty-five MSU.

Lo on Top

The greatest running back in Michigan State history was almost a Michigan Wolverine. Lorenzo White, a prep star from Fort Lauderdale, Florida, had his choice of schools, and Michigan, MSU, Tennessee, Georgia, and Pittsburgh made his final five. Then he cut the list down to the Spartans and Wolverines. His official visit to MSU, as a high school senior in the fall of 1983, made the choice an easy one.

"MSU stood out when I got there as a place that really, really wanted me," White remembered. "And I wanted to go to a place where I could stand out, make my mark. A place that when I left, people remembered Lo White. Georgia had its Herschel Walker already, I wanted to be that for Michigan State."

White finished four illustrious seasons as MSU's all-time leading rusher with 4,887 yards, despite playing sparingly the first half of his

Lorenzo White (34) toted the pigskin 56 times for 292 yards in this Rose Bowl–clinching win over Indiana.

freshman season and missing half of his junior season with a knee injury. White "had it all," said his coach at MSU, George Perles. Speed, power, vision, and moves, all wrapped up in a 5'11", 205-pound frame.

White, whose record is likely to stand for a long time, had plenty of highlights, including his 56-carry, 292-yard effort to help beat Indiana and clinch a Rose Bowl berth for MSU in 1987. But he says his number one memory is the 185-yard day he had against Michigan that same season. White was not yet in the rotation as a freshman when MSU beat Michigan in 1984. He played sparingly on a bum ankle in 1985 against U-M and missed the 1986 game with that knee injury. So he had to make the most of his only full-strength shot at his rivals—and near-teammates. "It's always great to beat your rival, and especially for me," White said later, "after never really getting to play against them before that."

White ran for 111 yards and two touchdowns, leading the Spartans to a 27–13 victory over Rodney Peete and the Trojans. Junior quarterback Bobby McCallister, the big question mark entering the season, acquitted himself nicely as a run-pass threat.

That set up a visit to number nine Notre Dame and another nationally televised night game. What was billed as the Heisman showdown between White and Irish receiver Tim Brown ended with a clear front-runner. Brown scored on punt returns of 71 and 66 yards in the first quarter, and he would have had a third later if not for a shoestring tackle. "I was stubborn and kept punting the ball to him," Perles remembered. "I wanted to knock his block off, but it didn't work. He won." So did the Fighting Irish, 31–8, as MSU's offense sputtered all evening.

Then things got worse. Number seven Florida State, featuring Deion Sanders, Sammie Smith, and a busload of NFL talent, was due for a visit to Spartan Stadium. The day before the game, Duffy Daugherty—a legend to all Spartans and a mentor to Perles—died of kidney failure in California at age seventy-two. A grim weekend got much worse for Perles on the field. After MSU's defense held tough for a 7–3 halftime deficit, the Seminoles converted a punt block and some turnovers into 24 second-half points and a 31–3 romp. MSU's defense had actually played well, but the offense under McCallister was going nowhere. And Perles was now getting booed lustily in his own stadium.

White's Heisman campaign was pretty much finished, and MSU's hopes of earning national respect were gone along with its national ranking. But in the Big Ten and Rose Bowl race, the Spartans were 0–0 like everyone else. So the team refocused, traveled to Iowa for a very winnable opener . . . and played like zombies for thirty minutes. It was all finally enough for Perles.

"Yeah, he used a lot of profanity to get his message across," remembered John Miller, then a junior strong safety. "But he had a message, and it was: 'This defense can be dominating if it wants to be.' We just had to find an attitude. And he gave us the attitude we needed at the perfect time."

The Spartans came out of the locker room with one thing in mind: inflicting physical harm on everyone in yellow and black. They turned the season in the process. MSU held Iowa to minus-46 yards rushing in the second half, pitching a shutout and securing a 19–14 victory. McCallister's touchdown pass to tight end Mike Sargent provided the winning margin. But it was that defense—fast, physical, and, finally, nasty—that was clearly on the verge of greatness.

The "Stunt 4-3" was Perles's creation, but this defense belonged to Nick Saban. A former hard-hitting defensive back at Kent State, Saban had made an impression on Perles in the seventies when he "hung around" Steelers practices, Perles said, and showed a determination to get into coaching. When Perles moved to MSU in 1983, he remembered Saban and hired him as an assistant. In his first season Perles went without a defensive coordinator, but he gave Saban the position starting in 1984. There was not a more determined, hard-driven, or foul-mouthed coach on the practice field in those days than Saban.

"He was extremely demanding," John Miller said of Saban. "He was the kind of guy—unfortunately, few of us really liked Nick. All of us respected him. I was one of the guys who did like him, he was a super guy off the field. But when it came to football, there's no more intense individual I've ever met than Nick Saban."

Linebacker Percy Snow (48) was the centerpiece of a defense that got stingier as the season progressed.

In 1987 Saban finally had all the ingredients necessary to construct a dominating unit. Up front, tackles Mark Nichols and Travis Davis started everything by disrupting opposing lines. Ends John Budde, Joe Bergin, and Jim Szymanski weren't stars, but they were relentless and stout against the run. Outside linebacker Tim Moore was a violent hitter, and his counterpart on the other side, Kurt Larson, "was probably the most underrated player on that defense, and maybe the best athlete we had," said

"Until You Bleed Inside"

When Miami Dolphins head coach Nick Saban made a player cry during training camp in 2005—in a moment replayed often on ESPN—no one who's ever played for him was surprised. Saban has always been a brutally demanding coach, and his refusal to accept anything but perfection was a key to Michigan State's 1987 Rose Bowl championship.

"He wanted everybody to hate him, because it gave everyone on the defense a common enemy: 'Let's band together and show that son-of-a-bitch that we can do it,'" explained former MSU safety John Miller. "We almost hated Sunday film sessions. I don't care if you just beat Michigan, you walked out of Sunday meetings and you felt like you lost."

MSU's 1987 defense led the nation in rushing defense (61.5 yards per game) and was number two overall (225.6). Head coach George Perles's "Stunt 4-3" worked to perfection that season, thanks to a group of talented, hard-hitting players and Saban's leadership. "He thrives on giving effort and making us give effort until it hurts," defensive tackle Travis Davis told the *Chicago Tribune* that season. "That's what he tells us—'You are going to have to go play after play until you bleed inside.'"

After successful stints as an NFL assistant, Saban replaced Perles in 1995 as MSU's head coach and went 34-24-1 in five seasons. His fifth team went 9-2 in the regular season, but he left for Louisiana State before its bowl game—a victory over Florida in the Citrus Bowl under Saban's replacement, Bobby Williams. Saban went on to win a national title with the Tigers before eventually leaving for his destined position as an NFL head coach with the Dolphins.

Miller. In the secondary, sophomore Harlon Barnett was an emerging star at one cornerback, and junior Derrick Reed was a huge addition at the other corner. Reed was a transfer from Southern Methodist, which had been given the death penalty by the NCAA for a slew of serious violations. His arrival gave MSU a boost at the one position where it was lacking. The safeties— Miller and Todd Krumm—were stars, delivering huge hits in run support and combining for seventeen interceptions that season. Krumm set the school record with nine.

But it all came down to Percy Snow. The sophomore from Canton, Ohio, was big, fast, and surly—and Saban's constant harassment only made him surlier. The key to Perles's defense is a rangy middle linebacker who can race from sideline to sideline and make plays. Snow, like Jack Lambert, was prototypical. "He was just a great player. He came off the ball like nobody's business," Perles said of Snow, a two-time All-American who became the first player to win both the Butkus and Lombardi Awards as a senior in 1989. "It was something special to see, watching him play."

The same could be said for the entire defense, after it found itself at Iowa. "I'd stand up on the sidelines just to watch them play," Lorenzo White remembered. "It was unbelievable, because you knew the other team didn't have a chance."

That was certainly true of Michigan on October 10. The number twelve Wolverines had not lost in Spartan Stadium since 1969. In that game Duffy Daugherty had mystified first-year U-M coach Bo Schembechler by installing the power-I the week of the game. Perles, in a nod to Duffy, put in a few wishbone plays to help the Spartans. But most of the help came from his defense.

John Miller (44) picked off eight passes in 1987, and four of them came in this 17–11 win over Michigan.

An early interception thrown by U-M quarterback Demetrius Brown and caught by John Miller was a hint of things to come. Miller later intercepted another Brown pass. Then another. Then another. Krumm had two of his own. And Barnett killed the Wolverines' final threat with a pick, making for seven on the day—and a 17–11 MSU victory. "I can't fathom that many turnovers. It's amazing to me we had a chance up to the end," Schembechler said after the game.

"The U-M linemen were yelling to the sidelines to Bo, 'Take him out! Take him out!' Krumm remembered. "There was no Michigan mystique on that day. They were breaking down."

White galloped for 185 yards, the most a back had ever earned against a Schembechler team. The Wolverines managed just 93 on the ground. And the Spartans, sensing that bigger things were in their control, did not treat the victory as a season-maker as some MSU teams have done when beating the Wolverines. The Spartans didn't let up either, coming up with a 38–0 revenge win over Northwestern the following week. That prompted the *Lansing State Journal* to run a contest for fans to pick an appropriate nickname for MSU's defense. Ultimately the *Journal* went with its own idea: "Gang Green."

Thoughts of the Rose Bowl hung in the air around East Lansing, but the Spartans also knew they needed more consistency from their offense. McCallister, who had struggled miserably as a freshman in relief of an injured Dave Yarema, was up and down. White had hit his stride in the Michigan game, and he was running behind a terrific offensive line, anchored by massive All-America tackle Tony Mandarich. Center and co-captain Pat Shurmur, guards Bob Kula and Vince Tata, and right tackle David Houle formed an effective unit. The question was, could McCallister open things up enough to keep defenses from stacking the line to stop White? "We do have a passing game," promised Rison, who teamed with Willie Bouyer to give MSU dangerous but under-used threats. "And once it begins to click, we'll be hard to stop."

It did not click in MSU's next game, a homecoming affair against Illinois. Heavy rain helped the heavy underdogs stay ahead most of the afternoon. McCallister tied the game at 14–14 by running one in, after his 34-yard scramble kept the drive alive. Then Krumm collected a crucial interception and returned it to the Illinois 15 with less than a minute to play. But standout kicker John Langeloh shanked the game-winning attempt, and the Spartans had to settle for a tie. There would be little time to dwell on the disappointment; a trip to Columbus, Ohio, was next.

It was a Big Ten championship elimination game. And MSU, back in the familiar role of underdog, took a punch from Ohio State on the first play from scrimmage. OSU quarterback Tom Tupa dropped back and threw deep to Everett Ross for a 79-yard touchdown. For one of the few times all season, MSU's safeties were caught sleeping. "I said, 'You've got to be [kidding] me. Here we go,'" Perles says. "I thought we were in deep, deep trouble."

His players didn't. "No," Miller said. "It just pissed us off."

Apparently. The rest of the afternoon was a showcase of one of the most fearsome defenses the Big Ten had seen in years—and it wasn't the defense manned by OSU linebacker Chris Spielman. After that 79-yard opener, the Buckeyes gained only 68 yards the rest of the afternoon. They totaled 2 rushing yards. Tupa was sacked five times by 258-pound tackle Travis Davis—an Ohio native who had been told by OSU coach Earle Bruce that he was too small to play at this level. And when the Spartans weren't popping Tupa, they were punishing star running back Carlos Snow.

"We had been reading a lot about Carlos Snow and what a great player he was," Krumm said. "I remember they tossed to him on one play, and John Miller came up and hit him. He folded like a deck of cards. We kind of looked at each other and said, 'This is the guy we've been reading about who's so tough?'"

McCallister passed for just 61 yards, but he ran for 83 and directed a 13–7 MSU victory. It was all very real now for MSU and their fans. This was it. This was the team that could bring the school's first Big Ten championship in nine years; its first Rose Bowl trip in twenty-two years; its first Rose Bowl victory in thirty-two years. "We knew then," White said. "It was like, 'Oh my God.'"

The Spartans' momentum was too much for Purdue, which fell 45–3 the next week. White rushed for 144 yards, backup Blake Ezor had 151, and McCallister showed signs of improvement in MSU's sprint-out passing attack. It was a satisfying victory. And it set up the most anticipated sporting event on the MSU campus in years.

It would be number thirteen MSU against number sixteen Indiana for the Big Ten championship on November 14 at Spartan Stadium. An upside-down league race would be decided a week earlier than usual, and neither Michigan nor Ohio State would have a say. "This is the thing we've worked so hard for," McCallister said. "Now it's time for us to cash in on it. It's right there. It's in the palm of our hand."

And there was no way the Spartans were going to fumble it away. Around campus, the week leading up to the game was more about planning a celebration than nervous anticipation. Meanwhile, Saban was preparing his defense so thoroughly for Indiana's offense that Spartans would be calling plays out all day before the snap. East Lansing was ready to explode, and a memorial service for Daugherty scheduled for Saturday morning only served to pack more emotion into the affair. Everyone who had ever played for or coached with Daugherty was there at St. John's Student Center—the same place the coach took his Catholic players before games—on that chilly, overcast morning.

Perles emerged from the service openly crying. He was cool and composed, however, at kickoff a few hours later.

The Hoosiers had no chance. The only threat MSU's players felt that day came after their 27–3 win, when thousands of fans poured onto the field to revel and attack the goalposts, creating a few frighteningly chaotic moments for some. Indiana star tailback Anthony Thompson rushed for 23 yards. White, in a fantasy farewell to Spartan Stadium, rushed for 292 yards on 56 carries—one short of the NCAA single-game record for attempts, a record Perles and White tried to attain before time ran out. "I said, 'Are you tired?' He said, 'No.' I said, 'You're a goddamn liar, but I'm gonna give you the ball anyway,'" recalled Perles.

"The adrenaline was pumping so hard I didn't feel it," says White. "But after that game? Oh my God. I had cramps in my sleep all night."

Amid the postgame hysteria, an ABC sideline reporter caught up with Perles, who took the opportunity to look to the sky and thank Daugherty. Moments later, with everyone safe and celebrating in the locker room, Indiana coach Bill Mallory burst in and gave a rousing speech. "Go win the Rose Bowl," he said.

First the Spartans had to wrap up the regular season with a trip to lowly Wisconsin. It was a chance to continue developing their passing game, and McCallister responded by completing ten of twelve passes for 200-plus yards. It was also an opportunity to set some defensive records. But Saban, thinking practically as usual, sent in the reserves midway through MSU's 30–9 win, and they allowed some yardage and a touchdown. It was the first time an opponent crossed MSU's goal line since that opening pass at Ohio State—an incredible span of 186 minutes and 20 seconds.

The Spartans ended up allowing 37.6 rushing yards and 184.5 total yards per game in conference games, both of which came up just short of the records. Overall, MSU led the nation with 61.5 rushing yards per game allowed and was number two in the nation in total defense (225.6). It was all very impressive. But none of it changed the fact that the Big Ten had lost sixteen of the past eighteen Rose Bowls to the Pac-10. And it didn't deter MSU's Rose Bowl opponent, Southern Cal, from openly seeking revenge for its season-opening defeat in East Lansing.

MSU knew it was in for a battle. Perles let his team live it up anyway. He opted for a posh resort in Newport Beach instead of staying in Pasadena like most Big Ten teams. He took the Spartans to Universal Studio and Disneyland and made an appearance on *The Today Show*. He encouraged the players to stay focused but enjoy the MSU fans—and there were thousands crawling all over California. When game day arrived, 55,000 of the crowd of 103,000 at the Rose Bowl were clad in green and white. And their team was relaxed and ready. "We knew we could beat them again," White said later of the Trojans, "despite all the noise they were talking."

A pair of White touchdown runs gave MSU a 14–3 lead. That's where it stood at the half, but USC quarterback Rodney Peete got hot after the break, finding the seams in MSU's secondary. His second touchdown pass to Ken Henry, midway through the fourth quarter, tied the game at 17–17. The momentum was all on the Trojans' side now, and when they stuffed a pair of MSU runs on the Spartans' next possession, their takeover seemed inevitable.

Thirty-Two Years Earlier

MSU's 20–17 win over Southern Cal in the Rose Bowl on January 1, 1988, ended a long, long wait for Spartan fans—a thirty-two-year wait to be exact. MSU's last Rose Bowl victory, another 3-point thriller, had been January 2, 1956.

Just as kicker John Langeloh provided the winning points with a field goal in 1988, Dave Kaiser booted a 41-yarder with 7 seconds left to beat UCLA 17–14 in 1956. The difference was that Kaiser, a sophomore end from Alpena, had not made a field goal all season.

Gerry Planutis, MSU's regular kicker, had missed two tries that day, so coach Duffy Daugherty went with Kaiser, MSU's "long-range" specialist. Kaiser had missed his only two attempts that season, but this one went through, earning Kaiser the nickname "Golden Toe."

The victory capped a 9–1 season and helped MSU finish number two in both major polls. An independent selector chose the Spartans as national champions. Daugherty's second team and only Rose Bowl champ was led by All-Americans in quarterback Earl Morrall, guard Carl "Buck" Nystrom, tackle Norm Masters, and Planutis, a fullback.

McCallister faced a third-and-8 from the MSU 36, and it was up to him to bail out his team. He took the snap and rolled to his right. The Southern Cal pass rush was all over him, forcing him to the sideline. It appeared McCallister was going to have to take

After his Rose Bowl triumph, George Perles (center) gets a hug from Michigan governor Jim Blanchard.

it out of bounds and leave things to All-America punter Greg Montgomery. Instead, just before stepping out, McCallister jumped . . . seemed to hang there for a second or two . . . and zipped a pass across his body to Rison, who had broken free in the middle of the field. Rison turned upfield for a 36-yard gain. MSU was back in control. The team's supposed weakness had turned in the biggest play of the season. "It was such a great play," joked Perles, "I said, 'We ought to put that in.'"

Langeloh's 36-yard field goal with 4:16 left gave MSU a 20–17 lead. And that's how it would end. The Gang Green defense would see to that. Southern Cal drove to MSU's 23, but Krumm pounced on a fumbled exchange from center. Miller capped off the evening by intercepting a desperation heave from Peete with 13 ticks left. Snow was the game's MVP, playing like a monster with 17 tackles.

The Michigan State Spartans were Rose Bowl champions for the first time in thirty-two years, and the third time ever. After twenty years of struggling, the program was back in the national picture, finishing with a number eight ranking. Perles had kept his five-year promise, and he did it without too many halftime tirades. He did it with a grinding offense and a bone-crunching defense. He did it with players like White, Rison, Snow, Shurmur, and Miller—players who could have gone anywhere. Rather than opt for the established powers of the day, they decided to reestablish one in East Lansing, Michigan.

"I picked George Perles," John Miller stated later. "Anybody can go play for a team that wins every year. The difficult part is going to a place that isn't winning, and then you go and help make it a winner. That's what we decided to do, and we knew we were going to get it done."

Upset Specialists

Starting with a 49–14 win over number four Penn State in 1997 and ending with a 44–41 overtime win at number ten Notre Dame in 2005, Michigan State went on a run of nine wins in ten games against teams ranked in the top ten in the nation. In the same span, the Spartans were barely over .500 overall.

So goes a program that has been up, down, and all over the place since the end of the Duffy Daugherty era. A variety of factors in the 1970s transformed the Spartans from heavyweights to middleweights—from giants to giant killers. In four decades after Daugherty, there were stretches of revival under Denny Stolz, Darryl Rogers, George Perles, and Nick Saban. There were great teams, in 1978, 1987, and 1999. There were great players, like Brad Van Pelt, Eric Allen, Kirk Gibson, Eddie Smith, Carl Banks, Tony Mandarich, Percy Snow, Lorenzo White, Andre Rison, Ike Reese, Tony Banks, Scott Greene, Derrick Mason, Flozell Adams, Julian Peterson, Plaxico Burress, and Charles Rogers.

And there were resounding moments, when unranked MSU teams toppled heavily favored, number one-ranked foes. No longer the talk of college football for seasons at a time, the Spartans had to settle for three amazing Saturday afternoons.

1974–MSU 16, No. 1 Ohio State 13

Coach Denny Stolz led the charge from the sideline, fist in the air, celebrating the biggest upset in Michigan State history. He had just seen a referee signal that time had expired with number one Ohio State at MSU's 1 yard line and trailing 16–13. As Stolz and the Spartans spilled onto the field, OSU snapped the ball, quarterback Cornelius Greene fumbled, and running back Brian Baschnagel picked it up and fell into the end zone. Another official signaled touchdown. The Buckeyes celebrated their escape and their twenty-game unbeaten streak with leaps and embraces around Baschnagel. For those few seconds, everyone was a winner.

And then? Stolz and the Spartans kept right on running—into the locker room. The officials were right behind, bound for an escape to their hotel, despite Ohio State coach Woody Hayes's

Surprising Saturdays

Here are some other notable upsets scored by Michigan State over the years:

- In 1912 Michigan Agricultural College and Coach John Macklin gained national notice with a 35–20 victory at mighty Ohio State.

- In 1913 and 1915 Michigan Agricultural College beat Michigan behind stars Blake Miller and Gideon Smith. The Aggies won 12–7 in 1913 and then rolled to a 24–0 triumph in 1915.

- In 1918 first-year coach George Gauthier scored a 13–7 home victory over Notre Dame and star player George Gipp.

- The 1945 Spartans, coached by Charlie Bachman and starring fullback Jack Breslin, upset Pittsburgh 12–7 and crushed number twelve Penn State 33–0.

- The second game of George Perles's first season, in 1983, was a 28–23 shocker at number four Notre Dame.

- In the final game of the 1997 season, Sedrick Irvin and Marc Renaud ran wild in a 49–14 blowout of number four Penn State.

- Quarterback Drew Stanton, a powerful rushing attack, and two goal-line stands helped MSU stun number four Wisconsin 49–14 in 2004.

best efforts to corral them. Fans poured onto the field. And the rest of the crowd of 79,000-plus at Spartan Stadium stood there . . . and stood there . . . and stood there. The scoreboard read MSU 16, OSU 13, with zeroes on the clock, but it wasn't until forty-six minutes after the chaotic finish, at 4:29 P.M., that a voice on the stadium loudspeaker made it official. The resulting roar "felt like earthquake tremors in the locker room," Stolz remembered years later.

Hayes was livid, barking at anyone who would listen and refusing to acknowledge MSU's victory. "Woody was out there screaming and doing his usual," Stolz recalled. "It was typical Woody; he had a terrible time accepting the fact that his team lost a game." Meanwhile, Stolz approached the podium at his postgame news conference and delivered the first question: "Is this game over?"

In the eyes of most outsiders, it was over before it started. This was a great Ohio State team, perhaps Hayes's best, with a crunching defense and backfield that included Greene, Baschnagel, fullback Pete Johnson, and, of course, Archie Griffin in his second Heisman season. The Buckeyes were on a nineteen-game unbeaten streak, averaging 45 points and 491 yards a game, as they headed for the usual season-ending showdown with Michigan. They had blasted MSU 35–0 the season before.

The Spartans, though, were showing signs of progress in their second year under Stolz. MSU's defensive coordinator in Duffy Daugherty's final two seasons, Stolz beat out the likes of Barry Switzer, Lee Corso, and Johnny Majors to replace Daugherty. After guiding a rebuilding team to a 5–6 mark in his first season, Stolz had his second team at 4–3–1, coming off an impressive win at Wisconsin, entering the OSU bout. Junior quarterback Charlie Baggett led MSU, which also had standouts in tight end Mike Cobb, defensive backs Tom Hannon and Tommy Graves, defensive linemen Greg Schaum and Otto Smith, and linebackers Terry McClowry and Paul Rudzinski. Graves and Rudzinski were freshmen. The defense had talent, and Stolz was confident it could hold the Buckeyes under 20 points. The question was, could MSU find enough offense?

"That was one of the best teams, in terms of personnel, to ever play in the Big Ten," Stolz later said of OSU. "The theme I gave to the team that week was, 'We can't just sit around and look at all that talent. We've got to find places that are weaknesses.'" Stolz figured the Spartans would have to attack through the air. If the Buckeyes had anything resembling a deficiency, it was their pass defense. And Baggett had some nice targets in Cobb, Mike Hurd, and Mike Jones.

Spartan Stadium was overstuffed and ready for history on November 9. And the Buckeyes, as it turned out, were ready for MSU's offense. The Spartans couldn't get anything going in the first half. But the MSU defense was primed as well. OSU scored first with a field goal, then saw three potential drives cut short by turnovers. Hannon intercepted a pass, and the Buckeyes lost two fumbles. MSU defensive end Mike Duda recovered the second one late in the second quarter, leading to a 39-yard field goal from Hans Nielsen. It was 3–3 at the break, which served as confidence-building evidence for the Spartans.

OSU drove deep into MSU territory to start the third quarter, but the Spartans held from the 3 yard line, forcing another field goal. Griffin was having a big day—big for most running backs,

Woody's Lament

"We won't know who won the game until the films come out."
That was Ohio State coach Woody Hayes's parting comment
after his team's 16–13 loss at Michigan State in 1974. Hayes
was convinced time remained on the clock when his team
took its last snap and wound up in the end zone. The Spartans believed otherwise and started running to their locker
room before the final snap. The officials agreed with MSU
and finally said so officially after a forty-six-minute delay.

Who was right? Who cares?

Big Ten commissioner Wayne Duke made all arguments
moot when he pointed out that not all the Ohio State players
were set before the final snap. That, Duke said, constitutes
an illegal motion penalty. And that, the rule book says, means
the game is over.

Hayes did not appeal the game. But he continued to com-
plain, pointing out that OSU had run one play in the final 26
seconds. The last official snap came with 14 ticks left, and
Hayes claimed MSU's players were trying to delay the game—
which should have prompted the officials to stop the clock
and restore order. "In practice, we can run four or five plays
in that time," Hayes said. "But in practice, we don't have people holding our players down."

at least—on his way to 140 yards on 23 carries. But MSU was keeping Greene from getting loose outside, and that was Stolz's top defensive priority of the afternoon. Now he just needed something from his offense.

Desperate to get the Spartans going, Baggett took it into his own hands on second-and-9 from his own 21. He found room on an option keeper to the right side, got the corner, and turned upfield. Baggett was all alone on the sideline, nearing midfield on what appeared to be a sure touchdown jaunt. He switched the ball from his left arm to his right—and dropped it. OSU's Steve Luke grabbed it at the MSU 44, and the crowd, standing and verging on explosion, sat back down with a sigh.

The Buckeyes kept them in their seats, marching down the short field in eight plays. Fullback Harold Henson's 1-yard dive made it 13–3 Ohio State with 9:03 to play. The Spartans, it seemed, would finally succumb after an admirable effort.

But Baggett wasn't conceding. Down 10 points, he had no choice but to throw, and the Spartans moved downfield quickly. MSU got into the end zone on a 44-yard bomb to Mike Jones. After a failed 2-point conversion pass, it was 13–9 OSU. Inspired again, the crowd helped MSU's defense hold the Buckeyes to three plays and out. The Spartans got the ball back at their own 12 with three and a half minutes left to achieve the unthinkable.

And they did it, with arguably the most celebrated single play in Michigan State history.

On first down, MSU called for "Veer 44." It was an option handoff play going right. Baggett was to read the defensive end and hand off to fullback Levi Jackson if the end stayed outside to confront Baggett. The end did, Baggett gave it to Jackson, and

Jackson broke through the line between right guard and right tackle. A juke left safety Tim Fox grabbing air. Jackson, a 5'11", 212-pound fullback whose fumbling problems had kept him on the bench three weeks earlier, found the right sideline and showed his startling speed.

"After I hit through the hole, I saw the strong safety coming at me and I faked like I was cutting upfield," Jackson said of the play. "That held him for a second and then I cut to the outside and I knew no one on the field was going to catch me."

As Jackson blazed along the sideline, his teammates trickled out onto the field behind him, doing their best to will him into the end zone. When he finally got there, he was engulfed in a wild stampede of Spartans, cheerleaders, and bell-bottomed students. "It was awful," Stolz remembered of the end zone scene. "I'm amazed to this day he wasn't hurt."

The stadium shook. The Spartans believed. The Buckeyes cursed. The scoreboard read MSU 16, Ohio State 13. The clock showed 3:17 left to play.

And that was plenty of time for an Ohio State offense that, for the first time, had desperation on its side. The Buckeyes started at their 29 and began to move. Griffin had the key play, ripping off a 31-yard gain to MSU's 40. Hayes had to use his last time-out after a play was stopped in the middle of the field, but OSU got to the MSU 1 yard line with 26 ticks left. The Buckeyes assembled and got the next snap off at 14, but the Spartans stuffed Henson's dive attempt. That set up the final play that officially never happened—and a wild celebration that, as anyone who was there will attest, most certainly did.

Levi Jackson's 88-yard sprint to beat Ohio State is one of the most memorable plays in MSU football history.

"We'd done a good day's work," Stolz said later. "They gave us no chance to win that game, and that's an understatement. It was a no-chancer."

1990—MSU 28, No. 1 Michigan 27

The hot-selling T-shirts around Ann Arbor that week said it all: "NO. 1 VS. NO ONE." Michigan was the nation's new number one team after blowing out Wisconsin and seeing Notre Dame lose and fall from the top. Michigan State was fresh out of the rankings after a disappointing home loss to Iowa. A contest that had promised to be competitive entering the 1990 season suddenly looked like a mismatch. The Spartans may have been the only ones who didn't see it that way.

"It didn't really make sense," remembered MSU star tailback Tico Duckett of the hype leading up to an October 13 visit to Michigan Stadium. "Michigan lost a close game to Notre Dame, then Notre Dame came to our place ranked number one and we had them beat [before losing 20–19]. Everybody thought Michigan was the powerhouse team, but we knew we were a powerhouse team, too."

The Wolverines boasted one of the nation's best offenses, with Elvis Grbac at quarterback, Jon Vaughn at tailback, and Desmond Howard and Derrick Alexander at receiver. And they took the ball and sliced through the Spartans on their first possession, taking a 7–0 lead. If MSU's talented physical defense couldn't do any better than that, this would surely be a long afternoon.

Then came one of the most important possessions of MSU's season. The Spartan offense, which had struggled miserably and received boos against the Hawkeyes, came right back at U-M. Quarterback Dan Enos took MSU 76 yards in twelve plays, capped by Enos's 8-yard scramble for the tying touchdown. Enos, a terrific athlete and leader, had some weapons of his own: Duck-

Hail to the Blockers

MSU heard all about number one Michigan's greatness in the week preceding its 1990 visit to Ann Arbor. More than anything, the Spartans were reminded of the Wolverines' massive offensive line, reputed to be the nation's best.

The defense took issue and made a statement by stopping U-M four times from inside the MSU 3 in the first quarter. And MSU's offensive line—left tackle Roosevelt Wagner, left guard Eric Moten, center Jeff Pearson, right guard Matt Keller, and right tackle Jim Johnson—made a bigger statement by paving the way for 222 yards in MSU's 28–27 upset victory. That was the most ever by a George Perles team against Michigan.

"Our offensive line is three times better than Michigan's line," MSU receiver James Bradley told the *Detroit Free Press* after the game. "Our offensive line is the best in the country. You can quote me on that. We beat them up."

The second-half numbers tell the story of a physical triumph. The Spartans ran for 152 yards in the final thirty minutes, against a defense that was visibly exhausted. The Wolverines, meanwhile, got just 55 of their 176 rushing yards in the second half.

"That's my program," Perles said later. "I don't worry about Xs and Os. Just knock their block off, win, lose or draw, and I'll hug you when you come into the locker room. Just knock their block off."

ett, bruising running back Hyland Hickson, and receivers Courtney Hawkins and James Bradley. And the MSU offensive line, led by guards Eric Moten and Matt Keller, established its physical presence on that first drive.

Then the defense got involved. The ferocious front seven, featuring linemen Bobby Wilson and Bill Johnson and linebackers Carlos Jenkins, Chuck Bullough, and Dixon Edwards, came together for a goal-line stand on U-M's next possession. The Wolverines drove down the field and had four plays from inside MSU's 3 but could not cross the goal line from the 1 on fourth down. It was a bit of payback for the previous season, when the Wolverines had stopped the Spartans on fourth down from the 1 in a 10–7 victory in East Lansing.

It was still 7–7 at the half, and the teams came out of the locker rooms and traded touchdowns again. U-M scored first, followed by a short pass from Enos to Hickson to tie it at 14. On Michigan's next offensive play, Grbac threw errantly into the arms of MSU safety Mike Iaquaniello. The Spartans finally had the break they needed to assume control, and the Michigan defense was visibly tiring at the hands of Perles's pounding offense.

MSU took eight plays to travel the necessary 69 yards. Bradley's sliding, 20-yard catch was a key, and Hickson capped it off by bursting up the middle for a 26-yard score. He ran through a slew of would-be tacklers and made sure to tell each one about it, then continued with a colorful display of trash talking in the end zone. The Wolverines could only stand and watch with their hands on their hips. Halfway through the fourth quarter, the Spartans were in command.

And that lasted for about 11 seconds. Desmond Howard took the ensuing kickoff, made a couple slick moves, and raced into the clear. He scored untouched, tying the game at 21–21. Howard's big play meant a brand-new ballgame and a revived

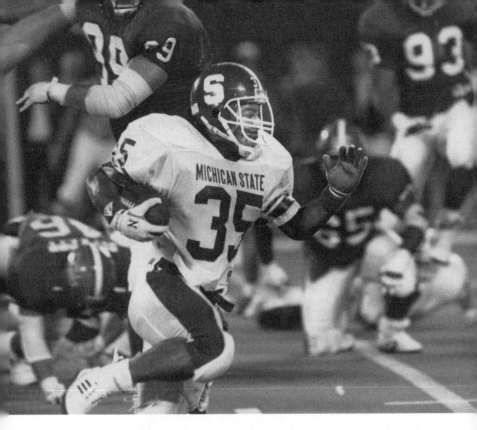

Tico Duckett (35) ran for 92 yards, and fellow back Hyland Hickson for 93, in MSU's 1990 victory over number one ranked Michigan.

Michigan Stadium. It also meant Michigan's defense had to come back onto the field.

Defensive coordinator Lloyd Carr watched helplessly as the Spartans picked up big chunks of yardage with the same running plays, over and over. Hickson and Duckett were mixed beautifully, keeping them fresh and U-M defenders flustered. Hickson ran for 93 yards and Duckett 92 on the day. "Whenever you've got two running backs with two different styles, that can be a real advantage," Duckett noted later. "With one of us, you're getting pounded, and with the other you've got to chase."

The Wolverines couldn't catch Duckett on the ninth play of MSU's drive, a sprint to the end zone through a giant hole on the left side of the line. The score came with 1:59 on the clock and completed a 70-yard march. But it did not finish the Wolverines. Grbac came out and threw thirteen straight passes against MSU's prevent defense. The last was a 7-yard fade route to Derrick Alexander in the end zone. Alexander grabbed it, and with 6 seconds left MSU led 28–27.

U-M first-year coach Gary Moeller called time-out to set up a two-point conversion try. That gave everyone enough time to catch their breath and prepare for a play that would go down as one of the most memorable and controversial in the history of the MSU–Michigan series.

Grbac took a quick drop from the 3. Howard, matched up one-on-one with MSU cornerback Eddie Brown, faked out and cut inside. Grbac lofted a perfect pass. Brown was beat, but he appeared to get a piece of Howard's shoe. The ball hit Howard in the chest anyway, but it popped out as soon as he hit the turf. Both teams looked around for a flag, and when the officials stood pat, the Spartans erupted in ecstasy.

Then as now, there are two distinctly different perspectives on the two-point play.

Howard: "When I got past him, he did what he could to stop me because it was do or die."

Brown: "He got into me first, grabbed me, and pushed off. I pushed him away, he fell, and the ball bounced loose. I looked around for a flag, and then I ran off the field as fast as I could."

Moeller: "You guys saw it. It was ridiculous."

Perles: "They have an argument. But Howard still could have caught the ball. All I know is, when the referee signaled incomplete, I was a happy, happy young man."

The Wolverines weren't done yet. They recovered the ensuing onside kick, setting up a Hail Mary opportunity for Grbac. His pass was tipped dangerously into the air near the goal line, but Brown grabbed it to end the threat. "No one" had just beaten number one. The Spartans lifted Perles onto their shoulders, a week after he had endured boos and criticism for his conservative offense against Iowa.

"We were playing for Coach Perles," Duckett said later of an MSU team that wound up in a four-way tie with Michigan and two others for the Big Ten championship. "We really wanted to win it for him. That group of kids would have done anything for him, and that's what that game was about for us."

1998—MSU 28, No. 1 Ohio State 24

Michigan State quarterback Bill Burke took the snap from MSU's 2 yard line and fell forward to the 3. Behind him, tailback Sedrick Irvin reached down and ripped a massive chunk of scarlet-and-gray-painted turf out of the Ohio Stadium end zone. Irvin then stuffed the turf into his pants and wheeled around to face a group of MSU beat reporters standing behind the end line.

"I told you! I told you!" Irvin screamed, his voice carrying into the chilly, suddenly silent evening of November 7, 1998. "I told you we were gonna shock the world!"

Burke took one more snap, fell one more time, and that was it. Michigan State 28, number one Ohio State 24. Twenty-four years after the Spartans ruined national title hopes for one of Woody Hayes's best Ohio State teams, they did the same to what was arguably John Cooper's finest Buckeye squad—one that looked destined for a trip to the Fiesta Bowl and a shot at the BCS championship.

More than one OSU supporter shed tears in the stands as MSU coach Nick Saban showed some rare emotion of his own, smiling and hugging players after the biggest win of his career. Whether or not the majority of his players had believed him, this was the scenario Saban had laid out for them six days earlier. "We have to look at this like it's a back-alley fight with the neighborhood bully," Saban had told his team. "We have to be the little, scrappy, scrawny kid who no one thinks can hang in, and knock them out at the end."

This was a maddening MSU team, one with plenty of talent on both sides of the ball but serious problems with consistency. The Spartans had a sharp junior quarterback in Burke, a star runner in Irvin, and two future NFL receivers in Plaxico Burress and Gari Scott. And the defense was strong, with Robaire Smith, Josh Thornhill, Aric Morris, T. J. Turner, and a little-known reserve end named Julian Peterson. MSU came in 4–4, with widely varying results to its credit, such as a 45–23 thrashing of number ten Notre Dame and a 19–18 loss to lowly Minnesota.

On the other side, no weaknesses were apparent. The Buckeyes had been tearing through everyone with a defense that included Andy Katzenmoyer, Na'il Diggs, Ahmed Plummer, and Nate Clements. The offense had a strong running game with Michael

Dotting the Buckeye

One of the staples of Nick Saban's five-year career as Michigan State's head coach was strong Ohio recruiting. Many of Saban's top performers came from Ohio, and many of them had been spurned in some way by Ohio State—making the OSU game as big as, if not bigger than, the Michigan game for those players.

In MSU's stunning 28–24 win at number one Ohio State in 1998, several Ohioans played key roles for the Spartans. Quarterback Bill Burke passed for 323 yards, despite completing just eighteen of forty-six passes. Reserve receiver Lavaile Richardson caught a 23-yard touchdown pass from Burke. Linebacker T. J. Turner got a crucial stop on a fourth-and-1 late in the fourth quarter. Turner and defenders Lemar Marshall, Courtney Ledyard, Richard Newsome, and Shawn Wright combined for 25 tackles.

And true freshman offensive guard Paul Harker turned in one of the game's underappreciated performances. Less than a year earlier, Harker, of Dayton, had given a solid verbal commitment to OSU coach John Cooper. But Cooper called around Thanksgiving and told Harker he was a bit light on scholarships; would Harker mind walking on at first? Harker minded, and he switched to his second choice, MSU and Saban. Injuries forced him into the starting lineup early in the season.

One of MSU's major concerns entering the game was Ohio State's interior pass rush, led by All-America linebacker Andy Katzenmoyer. Harker had troubles with blitz pickup early in the season, and his instructions here were clear: Leave your man whenever you see Katzenmoyer coming, even if you can get only a piece of him.

The results? The Buckeyes had one sack of Burke on the day—none from Katzenmoyer, who had four tackles. "Basically, I was getting knocked on my ass by Katzenmoyer all day," Harker recalled, "but it gave Bill enough time back there."

Wiley and Joe Montgomery and a devastating passing attack with quarterback Joe Germaine throwing to David Boston, Dee Miller, and tight end John Lumpkin. It all added up to the Buckeyes entering the game as 27.5-point favorites. "We were already down by four touchdowns before we even took the field," Burress said.

And they were actually down 15 points, 24–9, after Damon Moore jumped on a short Burke pass and returned it 73 yards for a touchdown with 9:51 left in the third quarter. The Spartans had done a nice job keeping it close and were driving for a possible tie, but the Burke error figured to be their final undoing.

Instead, Burke was able to shake off his mistake and lead the Spartans right back down the field. He hit Lavaile Richardson for a 23-yard scoring pass, and MSU was back in it, down 24–15 after Paul Edinger's extra point failed. On the other side of the ball, Peterson was almost single-handedly terrorizing Germaine and the vaunted OSU offense. Peterson, a junior college transfer and seldom-used situational pass rusher entering the game, was forced into every-snap action when star end Robaire Smith broke his leg in the first half.

By midway through the third, press-box inhabitants were questioning aloud how Peterson was playing behind anyone. He showed the speed and force that would eventually make him an NFL star, getting 4 sacks, 7 tackles for losses of 42 yards, and 3 forced fumbles. The Spartans recovered 4 OSU fumbles on the day—one of which set up an Edinger field goal to make it 24–18. Then MSU got the ball back and drove 92 yards, on the strength of some huge Burke completions. Irvin took it in from the 3 with 14:20 to play in the game, putting the Spartans ahead 25–24. The OSU fans was stunned, and their heroes were shaken.

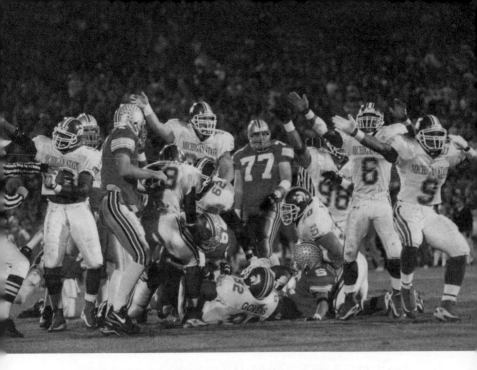

The Spartans help make the call after one of their four fumble recoveries of the evening. *Jesse Nieboer Prentiss*

"That's when it really started creeping into our minds: 'Hey, this can actually happen,'" remembered Paul Harker, then a starting guard and true freshman. "I don't know if the Ohio State guys would admit it, but you could tell, the way our defense was attacking them, they were starting to get intimidated."

Another fumble—by Germaine, after a Peterson hit—set up another Edinger field goal. With 9:26 to play, the Spartans led 28–24, and Germaine was simply incapable of setting up in the pocket. So Cooper decided to keep it on the ground. Starting from their own 19 on the next drive, the Buckeyes handed off eleven straight times and traveled 55 yards. With less than four minutes to play, OSU faced a fourth-and-1 at the MSU 26, and Montgomery got the call.

He took it up the middle and . . . SMACK! Ohio native T. J. Turner hit him at the line, fellow linebacker and Ohioan Courtney Ledyard helped drive him back, and the Spartans took over with 3:33 left on the clock.

"I'm at a loss for words," Turner told the *Lansing State Journal* afterward. "That's the play I've always dreamed of."

MSU's defense had been incredible, with 6 sacks and 15 tackles for losses. Aric Morris had 17 stops and fellow safety Sorie Kanu 12. Thornhill had 15 and Turner 14. Peterson was playing out of his mind. But one final, improbable stand would be necessary. After all that work, the Spartans had to punt with 1:51 to play, and Dee Miller took it back 26 yards to the Ohio State 49. Then Germaine connected on two quick-hit passes, one for 16 yards to Boston, one for 20 to Lumpkin. The Buckeyes had a first down at MSU's 15, the crowd was awakened, and the Spartans had to call a timeout with 1:29 left.

The inevitable was at hand. Germaine dropped back on first down and threw to Boston at the goal line. MSU cornerback Cedric Henry got a finger on it, enough to keep it from Boston's hands. On second down, Germaine overthrew Boston. On third down, cornerback Renaldo Hill broke up a pass for Miller. And finally, with tension at its peak, Germaine dropped and heaved for Miller, who was running an out pattern at the goal line. Hill read it, jumped in front, and picked off Germaine's feeble attempt. The Buckeyes, incredibly, were done.

"We've burned what could have been a fabulous season," Cooper said.

"I walked off the field shaking my head with a stupid look on my face," said OSU's Tyson Walter. "It's a bad joke. They shouldn't have been on the field with us."

As it turned out, the breakthrough would not propel the Spartans. They would lose the following week, in heartbreaking fashion, to Purdue and a sophomore quarterback named Drew Brees. MSU finished 6–6 with no bowl game. But the pieces were in place for 1999, when MSU would go 10–2, beating Notre Dame, Michigan, Ohio State, and Penn State and finishing up with a victory over Florida in the Citrus Bowl. And for one wondrous evening in Columbus, Ohio, Sedrick Irvin was a very satisfied football prophet.

"I told you we were gonna shock the world," Irvin repeated to reporters after the game, at a slightly lower volume than his end-zone outburst. "And if you see Lee Corso or Kirk Herbstreit of ESPN, or anyone else who said we'd be lucky to lose 41–10, give them my beeper number."

Drew
Attitude

Quite an inheritance awaited John L. Smith when he arrived at Michigan State in December 2002. The school's twenty-third football coach had come from Louisville to replace the exiled Bobby Williams, who had left behind some nice talent—and a fine mess. There was a dysfunctional team, one that began the 2002 season as a purported Big Ten contender and finished it 4–8. There was a glaring lack of authority and accountability, reflected in the way certain players ignored and openly disrespected Williams and some of his assistants.

There was a drug problem. Star junior quarterback Jeff Smoker had been suspended midway through the 2002 season and later revealed that he was struggling with substance abuse. He was not alone. Cocaine was a regular indulgence for a few of Smoker's teammates in 2001 and 2002—including at least two players who joined Smoker as starters and key performers in 2003. As one player on those teams put it, "There were a lot of drugs being thrown around, and it wasn't just Jeff, and it wasn't just two or three other guys."

There was a fan base fed up with thirty years of instability and uncertainty in the football program, many of whom were none too thrilled to see the previously anonymous Smith receive a six-year, $9.75 million deal from athletic director Ron Mason. There was a difficult recruiting situation with mighty Michigan, just an hour away, plucking the state's top talents on an annual basis—if Ohio State and Notre Dame didn't get there first.

At first Smith felt like he was trying to clean up the Exxon Valdez spill with a push broom. But he also identified a number of reasons—rich tradition, beautiful campus and facilities, passion and deep pockets from those same fans—the MSU football program could and should be successful.

And he found, amid the knuckleheads, a core of quality football players. One of the first who caught his eye was a freshman quarterback named Drew Stanton.

Stanton was redshirted and had sat quietly as the 2002 season devolved into utter disaster. But in the early months of 2003 he was a key figure around MSU's Duffy Daugherty Football Building. With Smoker's status up in the air, Stanton figured to have a

Born and raised in Michigan, Drew Stanton has been a lifelong Spartan.

great shot at directing Smith's new, pass-happy spread offense as a redshirt freshman.

A prep standout from Detroit suburb Farmington Hills, Stanton had all the preferred ingredients: size, at 6'3", 225; an arm strong enough to interest the New York Yankees in his pitching talents; National Honors Society smarts; and leadership that helped Farmington Hills Harrison High School claim back-to-back state titles. As a senior he had been ranked by every major recruiting analyst among the nation's top twenty quarterbacks, and he was recruited by just about everyone, including Michigan and Notre Dame. MSU beat out finalists UCLA, Oregon, and Northwestern for Stanton's services.

Of course, it wasn't really a fair contest. In the eyes of his father and brother, there was really only one choice for Stanton. His parents had met at MSU, where father Gaylord played baseball in the 1970s. He had spent part of his childhood in Okemos, less than ten minutes from campus, and grew up a fervent Spartan rooter—and Wolverine hater. Or something like that. "I don't think that necessarily I hate Michigan," Stanton once said in a moment of diplomacy. "I just don't like them very much."

He had raced to Spartan Stadium on a cold November day in 2001, after winning his own state playoff game, in time to see Smoker's toss to T. J. Duckett on the final play of the game to beat the Wolverines. Stanton joined a wild celebration with his future teammates. The next year, Smoker was off the team with his well-publicized problem, and Stanton watched helplessly as backup quarterback Damon Dowdell and the Spartans went down 49–3 in Ann Arbor. It was the program's lowest point in years, reached in mere months. Bobby Williams was asked afterward if he had lost his team. His infamous "I don't know" reply got him fired by Mason two days later.

Like everyone else on the team, Stanton was stunned by the coach's midseason termination. Unlike some, he did not revolt or look for another place to play. He made an immediate impression on Smith as a future team leader. And after 2003 spring football, where he had outplayed Dowdell, Stanton was MSU's number one quarterback. Smith had decided to allow Smoker to rejoin the team on a probationary basis, but he was not allowed to take part in spring drills, and he wouldn't be cleared to suit up until fall camp, if at all.

In August Smoker got clearance to play, which meant it was only a matter of time before he regained his starting job. Smoker played in his first game as a true freshman, had been brilliant for much of his sophomore season in 2001, and had the accuracy to do big things with Smith's offense. He was a no-brainer over any redshirt freshman, and Stanton knew this. But that didn't make it easy. "That might have been the toughest thing I had to deal with in my career," Stanton said. "It definitely forced me to grow up a lot."

It did not, however, keep him off the field. Early in the season, fans and media members began noticing a number 5 lining up as "personal protector" on punts, between the line and the punter. When he beat everyone downfield to make a pair of crunching open-field tackles against Rutgers in the season's second game, the first chapter of the Legend of Drew Stanton had been written.

"I'm not a sissy," Stanton explained with a smile when asked why a quarterback would volunteer for special teams.

"Kick It to Number 5"

As a redshirt freshman in 2003, Drew Stanton backed up MSU star quarterback Jeff Smoker. But he made a mark on special teams, leading the punt team with 13 tackles, 9 of them solo efforts. And he was in on a pair of huge, game-changing special teams plays as well.

In the season's third game, against Louisiana Tech, Stanton unwittingly became a key figure. The Spartans gave up two late touchdowns to lose, and it was possible only because Stanton mishandled an onside kick in the final minute.

The next week, MSU played at Notre Dame. After scoring late to cut MSU's lead to 22–16, the Fighting Irish lined up for an onside kick. Guess who they targeted?

"It's just common sense," Stanton said. "Line up and kick it to the kid who messed up." But this time, Stanton didn't mess up. He pounced on the ball, and the Spartans had their first benchmark victory under coach John L. Smith.

Stanton was a bit emotional after his grab. "You couldn't even give him a high five or hug him," Smoker said with a chuckle after the game, "because he was just flailing his arms and screaming."

"He's a football player," Smith said. "He's a big, strong kid, a tough guy. He'll be fine. . . . It's a great example. Here's a guy that's not supposed to be able to tackle or block. He's supposed to be able to throw the ball. But he's doing everything else. Maybe we can all do everything else. Maybe we can all do more."

While Smoker became a national story of redemption, smashing all of MSU's passing records and leading the Spartans to an 8–5 turnaround, Stanton became an amusing diversion. He led the punt unit with 13 tackles that season—playing with such ferocity that his teammates would actually get off the bench on punting downs to watch him go at it. "He was like an animal," MSU tight end Jason Randall told the *Lansing State Journal*. "He'd scream sometimes, like 'Aaaaaaaggggh,' the whole way down, then hit a guy with no regard for his body."

Eventually it cost him. In the first quarter of the Alamo Bowl against Nebraska, Stanton raced downfield on a punt. Nebraska's Ira Cooper caught up and hit him from behind. Stanton's foot planted, and he went down awkwardly. Stanton felt a pop in his right knee. Pain washed over him as Cooper woofed from above. And it took just a few seconds of Stanton writhing on the ground for everyone in attendance to realize that this was serious.

The Spartans lost 17–3 that night, but the torn ligaments in Stanton's right knee constituted a much bigger story. Smith's gamble had backfired after all. Smoker's chosen heir would need major surgery, would not be able to take part in spring ball, and might not be ready for the start of the 2004 season. It was time Stanton could not afford. Dowdell was ready to compete for the starting job as a senior, and redshirt freshman Stephen Reaves, a lefty with a giant arm, was lurking as well.

The Stanton family was understandably less than thrilled with their son's fate. But Drew refused to publicly blame or question his coach. After all, it was Stanton's idea to play on special teams in the first place. With his knee on the mend months later, he was actually still thinking about Cooper. Stanton was transitioning into a more prominent role with the team, and some of his first comments in that role shed light on the fact that he was a few notches more intense than some realized.

"I remember the guy over top of me laughing and talking trash," Stanton said of Cooper. "I've got his name. I know everything about him. For somebody to do that, to hurt somebody, then to stand over them . . . you kind of get that lasting image in your mind, and it's something that can't go away. That's something that motivates me every day. To make sure I'm at the top of my game and showing everybody that it was a cheap shot, and I will be the starting quarterback around here."

He was sure of that. Coach Smith gave no indication otherwise. But it was clearly not a lock as 2004 fall camp progressed. Stanton was still getting his knee drained, and Reaves was throwing lasers on the practice field. A couple weeks before the opener at Rutgers, Smith announced that Stanton's knee was still a bit wobbly and might not be ready for the opener. On the day of the game, Stanton let his coaches know that he could go if needed, but it was simply too much of a risk.

Dowdell got the start, faltered, and MSU lost to the Scarlet Knights. A week later, Stanton's knee was progressing, but the coaches decided to give Reaves the start against Central Michigan. And now Stanton and everyone else could see what was happening. Reaves was the only quarterback on the roster recruited by Smith. He was the son of John Reaves, a former NFL quarterback. He had the biggest arm of the bunch. And if he played well from here, Stanton might be relegated to career backup. The popular belief among media members who covered the team was that Reaves had quietly been Smith's Plan A all along.

Reporters asked Stanton that week about the prospect of never getting his shot. "If I don't, I don't," he said, revealing maturity and perspective to match his intensity. "There's a lot more to my life than football."

Reaves didn't become a Heisman candidate in his starting debut, but he didn't lose the job, either. Stanton got in some mop-up duty in the victory over the Chippewas, then he went back to his seat in Reaves's shadow. A Spartan Stadium night game with Notre Dame was up next. If Reaves could perform and pull out a big victory, his spot as the man of the present and future would be secure.

It took just a few minutes under the lights to see that Reaves was not ready for this stage. He threw a bad interception. Then another. Then another. He heard boos as he trotted off the field at halftime, and it appeared Stanton's opportunity was finally at hand. Smith tapped his shoulder as the half ended.

Things did not immediately improve. Stanton's first pass bounced about 5 yards in front of a wide-open Eric Knott, prompting Knott to throw up his arms in disgust. The MSU locker room was divided on the quarterback issue, and Knott, a high school teammate and close friend of Dowdell's, led the faction who believed Dowdell had earned the right for an extended look as a senior.

By the end of the evening, the Dowdell camp was rapidly losing supporters. After that shaky start, Stanton got things going, rallying MSU with his arms and his legs. He passed for 110 yards, ran for 49, and got the Spartans within a touchdown, 31–24. It was a difficult loss, and Reaves's failure disheartened MSU fans who thought he might be the answer. But Stanton's play was some consolation, and it earned him his first career start the next week, at Indiana.

The Drew Stanton Era began with a resounding thud. Stanton was so bad in the first half against the Hoosiers, everyone assumed Reaves or Dowdell would take his place to start the third quarter. Stanton was clearly still feeling some effects of his knee injury. He could not make the necessary passes to move the ball, and MSU trailed 20–7 at the half. A disastrous season loomed large.

Then an interesting thing happened at halftime. Stanton was not told to grab a cap and a clipboard and relax. He stood up and did some talking of his own. He apologized to the team for his play, praised his offensive linemen for doing their jobs, and promised to turn things around in the second half. "I thought that was great of him," MSU center Chris Morris said. "He said he was gonna lead us on the field, and he did. It's a great feeling knowing we can trust this guy."

Stanton did not magically locate extra zip on his passes, but he didn't need to. MSU's spread offense transformed, on the spot, into an option rushing attack. Stanton, who had never been known as a runner, kept leading option plays down the line, seeing the Hoosiers go after the pitch man, and finding himself running free in the open field. He ripped off jaunts of 43, 36, and 35 yards, spinning and breaking tackles when necessary. He finished

Option Galore

Drew Stanton's first start at quarterback for Michigan State, on September 25, 2004, also marked the debut of a new-look offense; the spread option. Down 20–7 at the half at Indiana, MSU decided to tweak its pass-happy spread offense with some option plays, and that suited Stanton just fine. He tore off runs of 43, 36, and 35 yards that day, helping MSU dominate the second half 23–0, for a 30–20 win. Stanton had been strictly a drop-back passer in high school, but his 12-carry, 134-yard day revealed an untapped dimension in his game and elicited comparisons to other great run-pass quarterbacks.

"Uh, no," offensive tackle Sean Poole said after the Indiana game. "He's nothing like Michael Vick." Maybe not, but Stanton finished the season with 687 yards on 96 carries (7.2 yards per attempt) and 5 rushing touchdowns—despite playing just five complete games. A full season would have meant 1,000 yards for the then-sophomore.

"I'm a slow white kid trying to do something," he joked of his running style, which coach John L. Smith often likened to that of a "drunken sailor." "I'm kind of running scared out there."

As a junior in 2005, Stanton ran much less and threw much more. MSU wanted to make sure he stayed healthy, so he ran for just 338 yards in eleven games. But he passed for 3,077 yards, with 22 touchdowns against 12 interceptions.

with 134 yards on 12 carries, completed some key passes, and led the Spartans to a 30–20 comeback victory.

While Stanton gave a TV interview after the game, a small throng of MSU fans began chanting his name. He acknowledged them with a smile and a fist pump. It was the beginning of a stunningly rapid ascendancy to full-blown stardom for Stanton. MSU football fans, starving for a reason to hope, had found it.

Three weeks later, Stanton became the first player in MSU history to throw for 300 yards (he had 308) and rush for 100 (he had 102 on 13 carries) in a single game. They came in a 51–17 upset of Minnesota, and with a trip to Ann Arbor up next, the attention of an entire state fell on the Spartans' sophomore quarterback. What was he like? Could he always run like this? Why can't he throw a spiral? Does he really hate Michigan?

Five days before the MSU–Michigan clash, John L. Smith explained to a captive media audience why Stanton was, in fact, always his staff's number one choice to run the show after Smoker's departure. "In the past, the best quarterbacks we've had have been the ones to show that linebacker temperament, that toughness," Smith said. "And I think us as a staff, we relate more to that type of attitude than maybe . . . the aloof, pretty-boy guys. We don't like those guys."

Any lingering doubts about Stanton were forgotten forever in Ann Arbor. He was brilliant, running, passing, and moving the ball with ease on the Wolverines' stingy defense. His passes were tighter than ever, a reflection of his ever-strengthening knee and confidence. He ran twelve times for 80 yards, completed ten of thirteen passes for another 95, and had the Spartans up 17–7, with the ball, late in the second quarter. That's when U-M linebacker

Coach John L. Smith took on a troubled MSU program before the 2003 season, but he also inherited a future star in Drew Stanton.

LaMarr Woodley caught Stanton from behind on an option keeper and threw him to the ground on a hard but clean hit.

Stanton did not get up. His shoulder had separated, and he lay on the field in a heap of agony for a few moments before being helped off.

"Their fans were cheering. . . . I think that moment changed him," Stanton's brother, Ben, later told the *Lansing State Journal*. "I think he left that field with a newfound determination—and a little more hate for Michigan, if that's possible."

Dowdell came in and played admirably, helping MSU take a 27–10 lead late in the fourth, but the Spartans blew the lead and ended up losing 45–37 in triple overtime. Stanton missed the next week, a narrow home loss to Ohio State. But he returned the following Saturday, taking over in the second half despite his shoulder and leading the way in a 49–14 dismantling of number four Wisconsin. Stanton was approaching uncharted levels of popularity in East Lansing, and not just with the fans.

"You look in his eyes," MSU offensive guard Will Whitticker said of Stanton, "and you know he's coming to ball like us."

But the Spartans did not show up as a team the next week, and a loss at Penn State—in which Stanton left in the third quarter after his eye was poked—eliminated them from bowl contention. The season ended with a bitter 41–38 loss at Hawaii and a 5–7 record. A potentially promising season had started and ended badly, with some tantalizing performances in between. The big victory, of course, was the discovery of Stanton, who had two more years of eligibility to help revive the MSU program.

This was now his team. As the Spartans entered the 2005 season, everyone hoped Stanton would be enough to offset a shoddy defense and uncertain kicking game. In preseason camp, Stanton's body was totally healthy for the first time in a long time; his passes were sharper as a result; and his command of the offense and his teammates was obvious.

"When he steps in the huddle, it's command. And if it's not

command, it's . . ." Smith said, trailing off and pretending to grab someone by the face mask and yank. "And that's what you look to see."

The 2005 season began as well as could be hoped. MSU offensive coordinator Dave Baldwin promised that Stanton would run less and pass more as a junior, in part to cushion him from injury. And Stanton came out throwing like an All-Pro. He shredded Kent State in the opener. He did the same against Hawaii the next week, leading a revenge victory and adding another entry in Stanton lore.

After receiving a late hit from Hawaii's Reagan Mauia with the game out of hand in the fourth quarter, Stanton left the game with an apparent bruise on his backside. But two plays later he raced back onto the field to break up a fight—or so he claimed— between Mauia and MSU offensive lineman Kyle Cook. Stanton stayed in the game, sending backup Brian Hoyer to the sidelines, and threw a key block on the next play that helped spring Javon Ringer for a touchdown run. Stanton pumped his fist lustily as Ringer capped a 42–14 romp.

"That's him, and that's the way he is, and you don't want to change it," Smith said of his quarterback. "You want a guy that's emotional. I don't worry about that, he's a great competitor, he'll fight hard. I don't necessarily want him out there breaking up fights and things, but that's the way he is."

He was officially in the Heisman discussion a week later. Stanton threw for 327 yards and 3 touchdowns at Notre Dame, leading the Spartans to a 44–41 overtime victory over the number ten Fighting Irish. He followed that up with five scoring strikes in a 61–17 laugher at Illinois. It was a full-blown frenzy

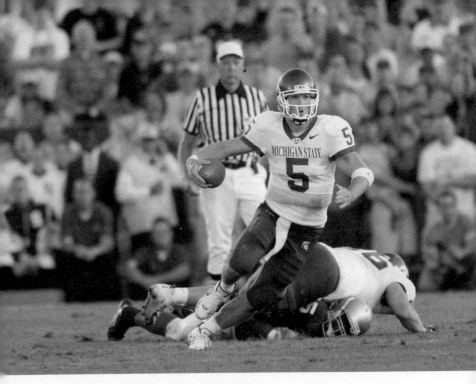

One of Stanton's biggest games came at Notre Dame in 2005, when he threw for 327 yards and MSU won 44-41 in overtime.

now. Stanton was sitting at 13 touchdowns to 2 interceptions, with 73.1 percent passing accuracy and the nation's top quarterback rating, prompting offensive coordinator Dave Baldwin to say, "It's just unbelievable how he's progressed."

Both ESPN and *Sports Illustrated* listed Stanton fifth in their "Heisman watch." *The Sporting News* had him fourth. *Sports Illustrated* did a feature story on him to set up Michigan's visit to Spartan Stadium the following Saturday. Everywhere he went, Stanton was in demand.

"I remember we were driving down the road, and people were yelling out of their cars, 'We love you, Drew! You're great, you're gonna win the Heisman!'" recalled Gordie Niebylski, Stanton's right guard and best friend on the team. "The thing is, it didn't change him. Getting hyped up changes some people—I'm not gonna name names, but I've seen it happen. But not Drew."

The wild success did not change Stanton. But it simply couldn't continue, either, not with tougher opponents ahead and deficiencies waiting to be exposed. MSU's kicking situation would soon be revealed as disastrous. And the defense simply couldn't compete with the Big Ten's upper-division offenses.

MSU came into the Michigan game ranked number eleven in the country and favored to beat the unranked Wolverines. But U-M took advantage of early MSU jitters to take a quick 14–0 lead. Stanton led the Spartans back to tie the game at 21–21 and then 24–24, and the game went into overtime at 31–all. But MSU kicker John Goss missed a short field goal in the extra session, Michigan kicker Garrett Rivas didn't, and the Spartans were perfect no more.

"I know I made some mistakes, unfortunately," Stanton said after the game, blaming himself as usual after a loss. "There were definitely some plays I know I could have made."

Stanton responded with arguably the finest performance of his career the next week, in a Big Ten championship elimination game at Ohio State. He sliced up the Buckeyes' NFL-caliber defense for 340 passing yards, and the Spartans were up 17–7 and driving late in the first half. But a coaching mistake led to a blocked field goal try and return for touchdown. Left tackle Stefon Wheeler's first-half injury and departure contributed to twelve sacks of Stanton, and Ohio State came back in the second half for a 35–24 victory. A plummet was imminent.

Fully aware that his defense had no chance of stopping Northwestern the following week, Stanton forced some throws near the goal line and came away with three interceptions in an embarrassing loss. "There's no question, he was pressing a little bit, because he felt he had to," Niebylski said. "And basically, he did have to." Two weeks later, Stanton cracked a bone in his throwing hand in a loss at Purdue. He finished the game and played the rest of the season, but the Spartans' fortunes were doomed, thanks to their increasingly helpless defense and inability to convert so much as a 30-yard field goal.

Six losses in the final seven games turned a 4–0 start into a 5–7 finish. Stanton went from Heisman candidate to no mention on the all–Big Ten teams. He and his team had been humbled, and he spent a good chunk of the season's final weeks defending his coach, who was under increasing criticism from fans and media.

"Coach Smith took a lot of responsibility for the losses this year, but there comes a certain point in time when the people in the program need to take ownership and step up," Stanton said. "And I'm one of those guys. . . . I think people are starting to understand what Coach Smith's philosophy is and what he's trying to implement here. It's being accountable and doing the right things all the time. And not just doing it when everyone's looking but behind the scenes."

That's where Stanton planned to do most of his work, lifting weights, studying more film, and increasing his role as team leader heading into the 2006 season. He would make sure everyone was doing the right thing. He would call out those who weren't. There was a lot at stake—perhaps including Smith's job security—entering Stanton's fifth year at MSU. He had one last chance to help Smith turn an inherited mess into a program on the rebound.

"Last season was another huge lesson for him," Niebylski said of Stanton as 2006 approached. "He learned to let the game develop, don't try to create plays that aren't there. And I know that as a senior, he'll just be unbelievable. He'll be ten times better, I guarantee it. He's gonna get this thing turned around."

About the Author

Joe Rexrode has been covering Michigan State University athletics since his time at *The State News* in the 1990s, and he has been the *Lansing State Journal's* award-winning MSU beat writer since 2003. Rexrode lives in Haslett, Michigan, with his wife, Katie, and son, Jack.

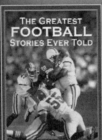